D. A. TEMPLETON

RE-EXPLORING PAUL'S IMAGINATION
A Cynical Laywoman's Guide to Paul of Tarsus

KO'AMAR
EILSBRUNN

D.A.Templeton, Re-Exploring Paul's Imagination

ISBN 3-927136-02-6

Copyright 1988 KO'AMAR
Verlag für Bibel und Religion, Maria Tanghe
Regensburgerstr. 11a, D-8411 Eilsbrunn

Druck: Aumüller Druck KG, 8400 Regensburg

matri meae,
    quae credebat,
        saltatorem in saltando,
            dum trans crus traiceret crus
                non jam surgentem, nondum cadentem,
                    ex aere pendere;
patri meo,
    qui dubitabat

To my mother,
    who thought that a dancer
        could at the apogee of his leap
            remain there and cross his legs;
And to my father,
    who doubted it

ACKNOWLEDGEMENTS

G.T.Griffith and Henry Deas taught me the little I know about Philip of Macedon and Pindar's Odes; Ian Henderson and Ronald Gregor Smith honesty and secularity; R.G.Collingwood that history is not what you thought nor even what you can remember; Ian Ramsey, both as a man and as a Bishop, how and on what occasions to begin to unpack and Rudolf Bultmann, by writing a Rite of Spring, as it were, against Elgar's Sea Songs.

A debt is due, too, to Kirsteen Moir for politely saving me from a Boeotian solecism by suggesting to me that I was thinking of something else of which I had no knowledge; to Father Joseph Munitiz, Editor of the Heythrop Journal, who, having excised the more offending portions of the early pages (the only ones he has seen), wrote me a sonnet on his blindness, believing, as a Christian should, that one should oneself admit to the faults of one's 'even-Christians'. And I thank Father R.C.Walls, who knows nonsense when he sees it and likes some of it; Dr. John Ashton, who likes less of it, but has an eye for Chekov and *Winnie Ille Pu*; and Dr. Carroll, who thinks that Plato had read Rabelais. Thanks are due also to Ms. Margaret Rankin, who typed my testament with a will; to a slightly puzzled team from Data Preparation, who usually know a *datum* when they see one, but were not always sure what they were seeing here; and to John O'Neill, who taught me more about *paraclesis* than about *paralipomena*: sc. he did not encourage me to leave out all I had written. And there was Tom, the Servitor, who picked me up early one morning off the Computer Room floor, like one of the more patient members of Squire Western's family in *Tom Jones*.

Not all the books that the Library contains could contain the praise for Mr. Howard and his Staff (let sun and moon bow down before them). Mr.Howard's ability to recall is only matched by his inability to be heard and his willingness to put a microfiche to his blind eye. He was always accommodating of access to the locked sections where Lawrence and Joyce are kept from the eyes of nascent priests, though Joyce is to be found also, be it admitted, quite openly in the Library Workroom. And Mr. Brown to whom the way up and the way down is one and the same was always ready with a *logos*.

But before all I thank Elizabeth, Kirsten, Alan and Calum. Hilarody, we are told, is a Hellenistic burlesque of tragedy, that replaces ululation with an archaic smile. It was Elizabeth and the children who had to deal with the hilarodist when after duties he went down-hill, late for tea. And a hilarodist that has gone downhill is not a pretty sight.

And I should add that for the blemishes that remain in this text, if there are any, there are many that are besides myself responsible, but that those above are not among them.

Stockbridge, Edinburgh,
8th November, 1987

NOT A PRETEXT BUT SOME LOOSE THREADS BEFORE STARTING

'This little book of whatever sort it is' (Catullus 1:8 f) is an address to the despisers among the cultured adherents of Christianity and started its life with the title or superscription: Peripsemata Postpaulina.

Peripsema is translated 'offscouring' (1 Cor.4:13 'we have become ... the offscouring of all things'). It and its plural form, peripsemata, may fairly be translated 'rubbish'. And in that half-world where Pauline theologians 'partly live' there occurs, at least sometimes, rubbish of a Pauline and sub-Pauline sort. More than justified recourse is taken to 'vain repetition' (and I here doubly commit the same fault) of what Paul has already said and what we have all already read and to critical discourse about Paul which is characterised by 'the rigidity, the coldness, the deadening effect of 'steno-language' (Ricoeur, 1978, pp.250 f, referring to Wheelwright, 1968, pp.25-29, 55-59).

Because I had (and have) no very great confidence that I had managed to do any better and not rather contrived to do a great deal worse, though the adjective 'postpaulina' tried to suggest that I tried to, I incorporated 'rubbish' in the title and tried to avoid it in the corpus of the libellus, the little book, the pocket-book, the pamphlet.

But the appeal of such a title to the man on the Clapham omnibus was likely to be very small. It would not communicate. Paulus in HHMoll ('Paul in BB <or Ha Ha> Minor') seemed likely to draw attention to the more risible elements of the text, but (again) was not likely to be sufficiently plain to Omnibus Man (even if some passengers on other omnibus routes of the global city might be prepared to extend a cautious welcome to it).

In the end my wife decided that no book that was to see the light of day in the second half of the twentieth century could dispense with the word 'imagination' in its title. There ensued a short moot, or what is nowadays, I believe, called a 'workshop', of a theologico-philosophical kind, and, the Ko'amar Verlag kindly concurring, there the matter rested: Re-exploring Paul's Imagination was what it was to be.

The subtitle has both a private and a public side. The private side need not become public, but on the public side it may be said that Diogenes the Cynic either debased or altered (both views are possible) the currency of philosophical debate and that it is as a man who made alterations that I allude to him. 'Laywoman' I choose for two reasons, first, to indicate that even ivory towers have, now and then, their seismographs: even in here we are not unaware of the feminist cause (though after the title I tire of the subject); and, second, because in the sixties I was schooled in secularity and the Layman is not a *homo religiosus* but a man as such and the Lay*woman* ... etc., and I do not think that the seam of secularity, though the accents have shifted, is quite exhausted.

Formally speaking, I should like to have produced a *catalogue raisonné* of Pauline thought. Which is admittedly a problem in so far as I have come to think that Paul did not *think* (he *imagined*), but all I have managed to produce is, more politely, 'an aleatory, open-ended collage' (I take the phrase from Gordon's Preface (p.vii) to Foucault (1980) and, less so, a *satura*, a *farrago*, a *pot-pourri*. The right analogy from painting would be *pointillisme* (though, I am bold to point out, the *pointilliste* does end up with a picture). But it is all too sub-atomic, even higglet-like (a 'higglet' is a very small particle <even smaller than Professor Higgs> which Professor Higgs thinks should be there, but has not been discovered yet). Of 'the desultory and unscientific thinking of our unscientific consciousness' Collingwood writes (1940, p.22):

> 'In unscientific thinking our thoughts are coagulated into knots and tangles; we fish up a thought out of our minds like an anchor foul of its own cable, hanging upside down and draped in seaweed with shell-fish sticking to it, and dump the whole thing on deck quite pleased with ourselves for having got it up at all. Thinking scientifically means disentangling all this mess and reducing a knot of thoughts in which everything sticks together anyhow to a system or series of thoughts in which thinking the thoughts is at the same time thinking the connexions between them ...'

Is there anything that can be said for fishing up, not an anchor, but an old boot, it may be, or a bedstead? But *Doth He that loveth the anchor not love the old boot also?*

Stylistically, Ps-Longinus tells us that 'speaking generally, tumidity seems one of the hardest faults to guard against' and there may be occasions when the reader will wish to introduce the writer to a Department of Rhetorical Oncology, where they deal with these things. I have tried to deflate the more tumid parts, not always with equal success.

A note too should be added here. This work is disfigured to some extent by what will seem to some an immodest concern with the dynamics of the genito-urinary tract, though there have been times, it will readily be conceded, when that tract has been very gravely undervalued. 'Arise, my love, my fair one, and come away; for lo, the winter is past ...' (Song 2:10 f): The Song of Songs does not belong to one of those times. But Aristophanes, treating Poseidon and Dionysus as he did, believed in 'the intimate association of the gods with the fabric of ordinary Greek life'; and the humour of the medieval Christian was 'full of casual blasphemy and prompt to interweave the comic and the tremendous'. If 'the Greek gods had human pleasures and understood laughter', if 'at the right time they could take a joke' (Dover, 1954, pp.100 f), does our God have none and can he take none?

The tone of some of the writing is brash, abrasive, has the 'convictional' (Zuurdeeg, 1959) tone proper to Sätze heiligen Rechtes, 'sentences of sacred law'. This is, of course, a misinterpretation and I would like the reader to preface each of such sentences with the rubric: 'It may possibly be hazarded that ...', or, 'it might tentatively be suggested that ...'. Or each such sentence might be punctuated by the Platonic parenthesis: '... or so it seems to me, at any rate' (has anyone written a thesis on the importance for the history of politeness of the enclitic γε, 'at any rate'?). But only Plato and Edwin Muir possess such charm.

What I have tried to say is perhaps threefold and may fairly be represented by the words, secularity, symbolism and metalanguage. Secularity is not very easy to sum up and anyone that wants to should turn to what Gregor Smith has written about it (1956, etc., etc.). But as regards Pauline language, both what Paul said himself and what is said about him, it might mean, I think, finding a non-technical vocabulary, what Ross (1981) calls an 'unbound' vocabulary, one that dispenses with many of the terms that have tumbled ripe (for 'ripeness', after all, 'is all') from the Pauline tree and have got quite squashed by the elephants who have been, for a long time now, grazing round the bole. I mean such terms as 'grace', 'redemption', 'sin' and other words of that kind. By symbolism I mean, I think, a non-historical use of language; language to talk about God and not man (in the first instance, at any rate); language that is suggestive; language with a wealth of overtones, which people like me are paid (but not too highly) to 'cash'. And all this makes Pauline language much more like literature than it is like history. Metalanguage, finally, is about finding a language to talk about Paul's language and my view is that such language is spread much wider than only in 'our field' and is not so much to be found in our 'field' as right over the hedge. In other words, literary criticism, literature itself, philosophy and anthropology, to name no more, may all be able to shed some light on the subject with which we deal.

In *The Church's Use of the Bible*, Nineham writes (1963, p.168):

> 'What I plead is that we should have some biblical scholars who come to their study from a background of professional philosophy and other 'modern' studies, and whose expertise is, if I may put it so, in the modern end of the problem. Perhaps in the light of their studies they might even do for us what Bultmann has tried to do, more systematically, and at the same time more tentatively and empirically.'

I cannot claim 'expertise' but only *interest* in 'the modern end of the problem'; and so, like Diogenes, if I cannot contribute to the defence of the city under siege, I can at least roll my barrel about a bit. Give or take some galimatias, it may re-assure the less muscular Christian or 'weaker brother' (1 Cor.8), if I say that my barrel contains only views that, while not much better, are not much worse than the views of Adolf Harnack, who at least in popular tradition believed in the fatherhood of God and the brotherhood of men — and we should nowadays add, the brotherhood of women.

Then add to these themes the benevolence of God (or 'benevolence': it is different from ours and when we speak of God's, we use ours as a model of it) and that benevolence as paradigmatically instantiated in Jesus of Nazareth. With that the mix is complete. When the crows (Pindar, *Olympians* 2:87) come about my thrashing pens, God peradventure will put half a dead rabbit in my talons.

But, however that may be, some degree of temerity may 'be ascribed to a book written in great part not (as Hegel boasted) during the cannonade of Jena', nor 'during the bombardment of London' (Collingwood, 1942, p.v), but in the doldrums of a régime upon which 'the end of the ages has come' (1 Cor.10:11).

Stockbridge, Edinburgh,
8th November, 1987

παραχαράττειν τὸ νόμισμα

change the currency

(The Delphic Oracle to Diogenes the Cynic)

Saint Médard est un grand pissard

'Making 'water is best' (Pindar,*Olympians*, 1.1.)
and Saint Médard makes it with the best'

O.Freiherr von Reinsberg-Düringsfeld,
Das Wetter im Sprichwort, Leipzig, 1864, p.141
(cit. Cook A.B., *Zeus*, III, pt.1, p.334, fn.2)

RE-EXPLORING PAUL'S IMAGINATION

A Cynical Laywoman's Guide to Paul of Tarsus

τὸ γὰρ δίκαιον οἶδε καὶ τρυγῳδία
'For what is true even comedy can tell'
(Aristophanes, *The Acharnians*, 500, cit.
Ehrenberg V., *The People of Aristophanes*,
p.22).

1.1. 'All men by nature desire to know' (Aristotle, Met.A, 980a22).

1.11. Some men some of the time desire to know what their convictions are.

1.12. A knowledge of the convictions of others may assist one in the formation of one's own convictions.

1.13. Paul of Tarsus had convictions.

1.2. The convictions of Paul are accessible to us from the letters he sent.

1.21. It is not true that none of his letters is available, nor that all the letters that have been attributed to him were written by him.

1.22. If it is judged that what Paul wrote God wrote, Paul's writings are called 'scripture'.

1.23. If the judgement is withheld, his writings may be called 'writings'.

1.24. Paul is an author of classical documents. Let us assume, as others have assumed, or found or claim to have found, that what he wrote repays study.

1.3. The historian studies the thought and action of men in the past.

1.31. The theologian studies the thought and action of God. He studies that thought and action in the past, in the present and makes guesses or is certain about what that thought and action will be in the future.

1.32. The theologian operates with three tenses.

1.33. Paul is in small part a historian. He tells us, for example, what Peter did at Antioch (Gal.2:11 ff). Paul is also in small part an author of autobiography. He tells us, for example, that he has been to prison (2 Cor.11:23).

1.34. But in greater part Paul is a theologian. His convictions are theological. He tells us that 'God sent ...' (Gal.4:4) Jesus of Nazareth, and so on.

1.35. It is arguable that the word 'theologian' is too theoretical to apply to Paul's writings. It is arguable that no thought ever passed through his head. It is arguable that what we have to deal with is Paul's imagination.

1.4. What the New Testament authors say about the activity of God has been called 'mythology' and classically called so by Bultmann (1953, pp.1 ff).

1.41. And so it is.

1.42. But 'mythology' is not the only word that can be used to give an account of the activity of God.

1.43. If we prescind from an examination of other New Testament authors and concentrate on Paul, what he says about the activity of God may be regarded as a constellation of 'qualified models' (Ramsey, 1967). The relation between God and Jesus may be modelled as the relation between a father and a son; and that model, 'father', should be qualified by some such phrase as 'in the sky'.

1.44. Such a qualification is there to alert the reader that some difference is to be expected between a father in the sky and a father on the ground. For example, a father in the sky, who is father of all is more philoprogenitive than a father on the ground.

1.45. To 'mythology' and 'model' may be added other cognate terms: 'image', 'metaphor', 'symbol', 'analogy', to name a few.

1.46. I do not wish to jump onto my horse and gallop off in all directions. I wish to have several horses at my disposal.

1.5. There is a difference between the elucidation of what an author has said and the repetition of what he has said.

1.51. There is a difference between the elucidation of what an author has said and the repetition of something some other author has said which resembles it. Two obscurities are not equivalent to an elucidation.

1.52. It is admittedly less easy to say what is equivalent to an elucidation and by what methods elucidation can be achieved.

1.6 Paul's mythology belongs to disused forms of language.

1.61. When an embassy from Athens came to Philip of Macedon in 346 B.C., 'Philip made leisure to devote to these Athenians on their important mission; and leisure he needed, for each of the ten spoke in turn and with all the conventional gambits of Greek oratory, not excluding the excursus into mythology' (Griffith, 1979, p.336). It is an excursus into mythology that is the very stuff of the present enquiry. The forms of language, that Paul used and we do not, need to be interpreted.

1.62. The symbols Paul uses can be closely correlated with the context in which he uses them. And that context has passed like a 'dream of a shadow' (Pindar, *Pythians*, VIII, 95).

1.63. That is not to say that there are not primitive survivals, that there are not aspects of the Pauline system that overlap with our own, for even now sons have fathers.

1.64 That is not to say that there will be an identity between the structure of the first century near-eastern Jewish family and our own. Indeed, there are some contemporary families that have no structure to speak of at all.

1.7. Paul is not being understood, unless one can say in one's own language what he was saying in his.

1.71. But is there any assurance that Paul in my language is identical to Paul in his?

1.72. 'The only assurance we possess is an empirical and relative assurance, becoming progressively stronger as conversation proceeds, and based on the fact that neither party seems to the other to be talking nonsense. The question whether they understand each other *solvitur interloquendo*. If they understand each other well enough to go on talking, they understand each other as well as they need; and there is no better kind of understanding which they can regret not having attained.' (Collingwood, 1937, p.251).

1.8. 'Every assertion about God', writes Bultmann (1952, p.191), 'is simultaneously an assertion about man and vice versa. So Paul's theology 'is most appropriately presented as the doctrine of man'.

1.81. 'If the premise is correct ...', writes Ogden (1961, p.173), 'then one might equally well conclude that Paul's theology may best be presented as a doctrine of God'.

1.82. Paul's doctrine of God is the subject of the enquiry here.

1.83. Or Paul's theological imagination is the subject of the enquiry here.

1.9. Bultmann uses the language of Heidegger to present Paul's doctrine of man.

1.91. I do not wish to use the language of Heidegger to present Paul's doctrine of God. This is not simply because the language of Heidegger is beyond my powers, but because the kind of resonance Heidegger enjoyed in the twenties is not the kind of resonance he enjoys in the eighties. 'The moving finger writes; and having writ, / Moves on ...' (Fitzgerald, The Rubáiyat of Omar Khayyám).

2.1. Suppose that Paul is speaking the language of 'the common sense and common nonsense' (Lonergan, 1972, p.53) of the ancient Near East.

2.11. And suppose, because Paul is a classical writer (1.24.), that he is also speaking the language of the uncommon sense and uncommon nonsense of the ancient Near East.

2.12. I wish to translate what Paul said into, I will not say the common nonsense, but into that *and* the common sense of the present.

2.13. And I wish to complement the use of that language by what Turner (1974, p.17) calls 'incursive nomadism' into disciplines that are cognate with the study of the New Testament, such as anthropology and literary criticism, to name but two. It may be that the study of Hamlet and the study of the Nuer can throw some light on Paul.

2.14. If it should be asserted that 'nomadism' is a denial of method, I should reply that there are contexts in which nomads can survive successfully and that there is always a time to move on.

2.2. Paul of Tarsus was a monotheist.

2.21. He can very nearly be called a henotheist, but he is careful to point out that while other gods are imagined they are imaginary.

2.22. Von Hügel somewhere asserts that if God remains perpetually incomprehensible he is infinitely apprehensible. The purpose of what follows is to throw some light on some of what Paul apprehends and on how he apprehends it.

2.3. Paul is chiefly interested in Jesus of Nazareth after the conclusion of his historical career.

2.31. He does, of course, tell us that Jesus was executed, but he does not tell us very much more.

2.32. To use a word of Whitehead, he is more content to 'enjoy' what is *now* going on than to remember what *did* go on. Nock (1964, p.27) puts it so: 'When the religion went further (sc. from the community at Jerusalem), the living transcendental Jesus could not but become more important than the 'Jesus of history': the Jesus who is the living Lord of the community is more promi-nent than the great Leader who had died and had been glori-fied'.

2.4. Arguably, it is the future that concerns Paul more than either the past or the present. Paul is pre-eminently a futurologist.

2.41. Paul constructs a picture of the future that contrasts with his experience of the present and the past. It is a picture in which the negative features of life are eliminated and the positive features are strengthened or idealised. It is *not* that 'the wolf will lie down with the lamb, but the lamb won't get much sleep' (Allen, 1976, p.25).

2.42. To allude to a passage of Isaiah (11:6), to which Paul does not allude, may serve to remind us that Paul is constructing within a constructive tradition.

2.43. Should the word 'construct' raise the hackles of the reader, the word 'occur' may be substituted. The imagery that occurs to Paul occurs to him in the way that it does, because of the way that identical or analogous imagery has occurred to Paul's predecessors.

2.5. The pictures that Paul uses have often been read literally, but there is no reason to suppose that Paul has been as unsophisti-cated as some of his readers have been. Realism is not the only school of art. There have also been idealists, impressionists, cubists and surrealists (I will not say with what school Paul's oeuvre is analogous).

2.51. 'The commonest fault of the pious souls has been', writes Hébert (1899, p.20, cit. Vidler, 1970, p.67), 'the taking literally the metaphors and symbols of our sacred books. The Oriental style misled certain minds inclined to seek before all things scientific rigour, or too much accustomed to logical formalism. They failed to distinguish between parable and history; they thought they saw astronomical and geological theses in pages destined to develop the religious and moral life of the soul.'

2.52. To use a word of Wilder (1982, p.166) Paul's mind inhabits not only the everyday, but an 'oneiric' world. belonging to dreams

2.53. But there are dreams and dreams. And Paul's dreams can be distinguished from the dreams of the Book of Revelation.

2.54. Paul repeats or plays variations on the fictive acts of his pred-ecessors and performs some fictive acts of his own.

2.55. Fiction, of course, is not to be contrasted with truth. The au-thor of fiction, Aristotle tells us (*Poetics* 1451b), tells us not what happened but the sort of things that may happen. Jesus was *inter alia* an author of narrative fiction; if we write off fiction, it follows that we write off his.

2.56. But those two ways of telling the truth, the truth of art and the truth of history, are not to be confused.

2.6. Jesus told stories.

2.61. And there is a story told *about* Jesus: that there is a world which has gone wrong; that Jesus has begun to put it right; and that that process will be completed.

2.62. The story about Jesus is one that Paul does not so much re-count as assume. More: he refers to it, he alludes to it.

2.63. The big story, the story about disaster and reversal, contains a number of little stories or sub-plots. Abraham and Sarah produced a child against the odds (Rom.4:19: 'He (sc. Abraham) did not weaken in faith when he considered his own body, which was as good as dead because he was a hundred years old, or when he considered the barrenness of Sarah's womb'). Moses' legislative activity was illuminating for himself and for the society for whom he produced laws (2 Cor.3:7: 'Now if the dispensation of death, carved in letters on stone, came with such splendour that the Israelites could not look at Moses' face because of its brightness, fading as this was ...'). Again, Paul refers to, alludes to these; and to others of a like kind.

2.7. Paul is a highly antithetical writer. He loves such contrasts as that between 'life' and 'death'.

2.71. 'Life' and 'death' are at least *prima facie* intelligible. There are other antitheses which are not, such as 'sin' and 'grace', 'law' and 'faith', 'flesh' and 'spirit'. I will return to these.

2.72. But let me 'loiter' to use Ramsey's word (1965, p.56) with 'sin'.

2.8. A religious context (I am speaking of the Christian religion) is a context in which the word, 'God', explicitly or implicitly appears.

2.81. 'Exhaustive treatments are exhausting' (Lucas, 1970, p.2). More can be said about the Christian religion, but I am not saying it here.

2.82. There are a number of words which can as easily appear in secular as in religious contexts. 'Life' is one of these and 'death' is another.

2.83. There are also a number of words that can only appear in religious contexts. 'Sin' is one of these. If there is a genus of specifically religious words, 'sin' belongs to one of its species. 'Sin' belongs not to 'unbound', but to 'craftbound' discourse (Ross, 1981, pp.158 ff).

2.84. Such religious words may be useful shorthand, but they are only useful to someone who knows what they are short for. Many people have forgotten the longer story or account, if they ever knew it.

2.9. These religious words may as well be described as the technical words of religion.

2.91. Philosophy is the attempt to be wise about anything whatsoever. Theology is the attempt to be wise about God; is the attempt, if you like, to be philosophical about God.

2.92. 'In philosophical literature', writes Collingwood (1933, p.202), 'technical terms are regarded with some suspicion. They are slightingly described as jargon, and philosophers who use them much are derided as pedants or criticised for evading the duty of explaining themselves and the even more urgent task of understanding themselves.'

2.93. Loisy speaks of 'notre patois théologique' (1903, p.68), 'the dialect of us theologians'. But a patois needs a glossary.

3.1. In the christian religion (as in many others) theology is correlative with anthropology (1.8., 1.81.).

3.11. 'Sin' is a word that describes the relation between man and God, when there is something wrong with that relation.

3.12. 'Sin' has a forensic analogue: crime.

3.13. Neurosis and psychosis are psychological analogues.

3.14. Filth is a physical analogue. And filth can be removed by a bath.

3.15. These are components of what Ricoeur (1969) calls 'the symbolism of evil'.

3.2. Bonhoeffer (1959, p.109) speaks of 'the non-religious interpretation of religious concepts'. Whether or not the remarks above are faithful to what Bonhoeffer meant, they are faithful to what I take Bonhoeffer to mean.

3.3. Semantic fields can be classified, for example, the forensic and the familial. 'Judge', 'crime', 'criminal' belong to the first; 'father', 'son', 'brother' to the second.

3.31. In so far as 'justification' is a forensic term, it can be translated 'acquittal'.

3.32. The word, 'faith', can belong to the field of personal relations. In this sense, 'trust' is a synonym. Friends trust friends; friends are trustworthy.

3.33. If 'justification' and 'faith' mean what they can mean in the phrase, 'justification by faith', then Paul is conflating two semantic fields: the forensic and the personal. Man, Paul imagines, is 'acquitted by trust'.

3.4. If the acquittal in question is the acquittal of a criminal, Paul is using a forensic paradox. The judge is acting illegally, except, I suppose, in the case where it is legal, where it is within the judge's rights to exercise a prerogative of mercy.

3.41. If the judge is behaving as an unjust judge (so Dodd, 1932, p.52), Paul is using forensic terminology to make a personal point. 'The judge acquits the criminal' is the forensic equivalent of the familial phrase 'the father forgives the son'. To use a distinction of Wittgenstein, the 'surface grammar' is legal: the 'depth grammar' is familial.

3.5. The antithesis between 'justification by faith' and 'justification by works' is obscure. If we retain Paul's terminology or the usual translation of Paul's terminology, the matter can be put more clearly by contrasting 'justification by faith in *my* works' with 'justification by faith in *God*'s works'. The contrast between 'the judge will pardon me, because I am innocent' and *'Dieu (le juge) me pardonnera; c'est son métier'* (Heine), or 'this judge will acquit me, though I am guilty', or, if theologoumena properly come not in one tense, but in three, 'God has acquitted, *does* acquit ...

3.51. Or the antithesis is between having self-confidence and finding that one has grounds for confidence that lie outside oneself. God's non-judgemental activity inspires confidence. His activity is not judgemental, but paternal.

3.6. From the fact, if it is a fact, that 'justification' may at least sometimes be read as 'the judge acquits the criminal', that legal language is, as it stands, not 'apt currency' (Ramsey, *passim*) for theology, that language from the legal field cannot be transferred to the theological without strain, without the need for some kind of re-adjustment, it is important to keep in mind that some other or all other such transfers may not be possible without some re-adjustment. *Omne simile claudicat,* 'all similes limp' (Straub, 1937, p.18).

3.7. Parenthetically, it is arguable (and Loisy, 1935, p.10 argues it) that, in so far as Paul's view is based on the interpretation of the text 'Abraham believed and it was reckoned to him as righteousness' (Gen.15:6), it is based on a mistake. For 'the sense is: Abraham's faith was imputed to his good works' (Loisy, *ibid.*).

3.71. Or is God making an assessment of his own actions? Or is God making a positive assessment of Abraham's assessment, that he, Abraham, has nothing positively to be assessed, or of Abraham's assessment that God has a good deal that may positively be assessed? Abraham has no childern and he is told that he will get some; no, many. Is to believe to act? Do I deserve to be congratulated, if I become convinced of something?

3.72. Whether or not Loisy is right to say what he has said, he is right to go on to say that the question is of little importance; what matters is not our opinion of the text, but Paul's. If we are after authorial intention, it is Paul's intention we are after.

3.73. Writing on 'O death where is thy victory?' (1 Cor.15:55), where Paul makes mincemeat of Hosea, Barrett (1971, p.383) observes that there at least Paul is not 'grounding an argument upon Scripture, but writing freely, in scriptural language ...'. Here at least also? And how often elsewhere too?

3.8. To resume before the parenthesis (3.6.), it would probably be instructive to know as much as posssible about what went on in law-courts in the society of which Paul was a member; to know, as it were, how 'acquittal' behaves on the ground before it gets into the air. By studying this we would be able to make a more or less accurate measurement of the re-ajustment demanded by the transfer of this legal term from the legal field to the theological.

3.81. It would be instructive too to explore the antecedents of Paul's society.

3.82. And, of course, his theological antecedents. For he stands in, is parasitic upon, a tradition, in which many terms have already been 'enskied' (Steinberg, 1984, p.4).

3.83. One might also make some kind of inventory of post-Pauline developments, in order to discriminate those features of that development that throw light on what Paul has said from those that conspire to obscure it.

3.9. This transfer is not one that Paul knew he was making. It is one that I know he was making.

3.91. Paul, in his writing, makes use of a number of metaphors of which he could have told us that he was using them. In offering 'milk' to the Corinthian 'children' (1 Cor.3:1 f) he is using the language of paediatrics or post-natal care.

3.92. Bultmann (1910, pp.88 ff) makes an inventory of these.

3.93. But Bultmann does not include the verba forensia, the 'forensic terms'. They do not, to repeat, belong in a list of metaphors that Paul (or Bultmann for that matter) knew he was using, but in a list that I know he was using.

4.1. These legal terms are metaphors in theology, if their literal use can be restricted to those cases where one man has a legal dispute with another man and cannot be extended to cover the case where the divine judge, God, has a legal dispute with humanity, with a part of humanity or with all of it.

4.11 This raises the question whether there are any literal statements in theology.

4.12. Jüngel (1974) finds one: 'God is God', and Ogden (1982, p.142) finds two: 'God is being itself' and 'God is a being'. Jüngel's statement looks to Jüngel like a statement that states nothing. And Ogden's first statement seems to me to violate the rules of the English language, but may be none the worse for that.

4.13. I leave the question (4.11.) as a question, for I am not one *nil actum credens, si quid superesset agendum*, 'thinking nothing done, should anything remain to be done'. *Vixerunt fortes ...Vivent fortiores?* Strong men have lived. Let stronger men arise.

4.2. Christianity is the attempt metaphysically to validate philanthropy, an attempt that coheres around the career of Jesus of Nazareth as a philanthropic man.

4.21. Paul calls Jesus 'christ'.

4.22. In all probability he was not the first to have done so. Certainly he is not the last to have done so.

4.23. If he is not the first to have done so, it is possible that he did not much reflect on the grammar of doing so. It is often enough said that the word 'christ' in Paul is etiolated, *verblaßt*, is pale and spectre-thin, survives only as a surname.

4.24. *If* Paul did not reflect on the grammar of 'christ', we *can*.

4.25. If the grammar of 'acquittal' requires to be supplemented by the judge who acquits and the criminal who is acquitted, the grammar of 'christ' requires an act of anointing and an agent who anoints.

4.26. Is it fair to say that the practice of anointing is fundamentally or at least originally cosmetic? There are occasions on which perfume is called for. And the olfactory is a powerful sense: from Cleopatra's barge 'a strange invisible perfume hits the sense of the adjacent wharfs' *(Antony and Cleopatra, 11,ii)* and there is Paul's fragrance from 'death to death' and from 'life to life' (2 Cor.2:16). Among comments that are less laconic Bultmann (1976, p.68, fn.8) remarks, 'the devil stinks'. There is an olfactory gateway to transcendence, be it from an aftermath or coronation oil.

4.3. It would no doubt be incomplete, but complete enough for my purposes, to say that with respect to Paul's antecedents, it is prophets, priests and kings who are anointed.

4.31. What kings are is clear enough, but the notion could be further clarified by a historical analysis of the Israelite monarchy and literary analysis of those texts that suggest that improvements can be made on historical experience, that speak of an ideal king.

4.32. Prophets are more obscure. They have been called 'poets' (Auld, 1983) or 'certainly poets, probably intellectuals, and possibly ideologues' (Carroll, 1983).

4.33. Priests are some kind of functionaries in the religious sphere, but we cannot appeal to the religious sphere, if it is the religious sphere on which we are trying to shed light. But if 'by ritual the anthropologist understands an organized technique, approved by the society concerned, for dealing with the incalculable element in any critical situation of human life' (Marett, 1933, p.1), then we may say that a priest is anyone appointed to use such a technique.

4.4. To 'anoint' (4.25) is to put oil or perfume or perfumed oil on someone.

4.41. 'Zadok the priest', Handel tells us, 'and Nathan the prophet anointed Solomon king' (cf. 1 Kings 1:34,39).

4.42. The anointing of Solomon by Zadok and Nathan is probably a historical event. To say of Jesus that he was anointed is to use of him a coronation or an ordination model or both.

4.5. If we prescind from the suggestive particularity of coronation and ordination, we can content ourselves with the rather general notion of Jesus as a leader. That notion, too, may demand some re-adjustment in the light of those historical facts we have or can infer about Jesus and of the demand those historical facts make upon theology, for 'the Son of man also came not to be served, but to serve' (Mk.10:45). Whether or not the statement was truly made by Jesus, the facts we do have suggest that the statement can be truly made of him. There are difficulties, of course. Are we sure that Jesus served the religious authorities of his day? But the difficulties are not perhaps insuperable. To what extent can allowance be made for what might be called Jesus' 'dualist philosophy'? Jesus belonged to a culture that supposed a symmetrical balance between acceptance and rejection, but it is hard to see how 'the love of enemies' can permit such a symmetry to persist. Is four hundred and ninety one the theological number that follows seventy times seven?

4.51. However that may be, the paradoxical nature of Jesus' leadership and God's leadership is classically expressed by Whitehead (1979, p.343): 'There is, however, in the Galilean origin of Christianity yet another suggestion which does not fit very well with any of the three main strands of thought. It does not emphasize the ruling Caesar, or the ruthless moralist, or the unmoved mover. It dwells upon the tender elements in the world, which slowly and in quietness operate by love; and it finds purpose in the present immediacy of a kingdom not of this world. Love neither rules, nor is it unmoved; also it is a little oblivious as to morals ...' And Whitehead's or Mark's or Jesus' view is implicitly and explicitly supported by Paul's redescription of life as death. To conflate with Paul the synoptic saying about serving, to serve means serving even if you lose your life in doing so.

4.52. It is not relevant here, but one may add all the same, that Paul is true to his antithetical nature by also redescribing death as life, a redescription that is aided by his redescription of death as sleep.

4.6. There are leaders and leaders. We have had some better than others and we can imagine others still better than the former. An idealising imagination belongs to the epistimology of religion. The historical imagination can grasp in some measure that which might have been otherwise. But we can imagine also that which might be otherwise (and *then* we may be prompted to assert that it *will* be). If we know of those who have won less wars than David, we can imagine someone else winning more. Is it possible to imagine the winning of all wars whatsoever, someone who puts 'all enemies under his feet' (1 Cor.15:25)?

4.7. Paul 'redescribes' (Ricoeur, 1978, pp.216 ff) Jesus of Nazareth dead as alive.

4.71. Paul imagines that he is related to Jesus of Nazareth, whom he has so redescribed.

4.72. That relation is modelled as familial; more precisely, as fraternal: Jesus is Paul's elder brother, 'the first-born among many brethren' (Rom.8:29). (The 'is' is metaphorical.)

4.8. Paul says that Jesus 'lives in him' (Gal.2:20).

4.81. Paul's prepositions are famous and notorious. The understanding of the preposition, 'in', that precedes 'him' is not much aided by the fact that it follows 'lives'.

4.82. If we imagine that Paul is a house and that Jesus is a potential resident, we may imagine that the potential resident has become actual. But we would imagine this more convincingly, if we had here a verb that more specifically meant 'reside'. Or Paul is a container in which Jesus is contained (Lakoff and Johnson, 1980, pp.29 ff).

4.83. Paul can wish, for example (and in theology wishes can easily pass for facts), that Jesus should 'pitch his tent on him' ('may rest upon me' <2 Cor.12:9>). This makes Paul not a house, but a piece of ground. One may be forgiven for thinking that the pegs were well hammered in.

4.84. A paraphrase can only weaken the original, but a man may be vivified by a vital companion. And it is possible that a dead man redescribed as alive possesses greater vitality than a living man so described.

4.9. Paul says that he has been 'crucified with Christ' (Gal.2:19). In point of historical fact, when he was writing this, he was not.

4.91. At this point in Paul's career, Paul had not literally been crucified, whatever may or may not have happened to him later. Paul is appropriating for himself language that was appropriate to Jesus.

4.92. Paul certainly means also that he is related to a man who had been executed by the Romans.

4.93. He certainly means also that there is that in his experience which makes 'crucifixion' a valid metaphor to describe it. Kamlah (1963) analyses some of these experiences and, for example in the catalogue of events, beating, imprisonment, travel difficulties and the like (2 Cor.11:23 ff), Paul refers to some of them.

4.94. But that is not Paul's point in Gal.2:19 (4.9.). Paul thinks that as a Christian he can play merry hell with the law. The law is an ass; not altogether an ass, but an ass nonetheless.

4.95. If a dead man cannot play merry hell with the law, because he is not there to do so, neither can the law play merry hell with him and for the same reason.

4.96. If one takes Jesus seriously, Paul seems to be saying, there is nothing else that need be taken seriously. This is Paul's philosophy of 'as if': one has things 'as if' one had them not (1 Cor.7:29).

4.97. 'Crucifixion' is a metaphor; the 'vehicle' is crucifixion and the 'tenor' is renunciation (Martin, 1975, p.205). The vehicle takes the form it does, because the end of Jesus' life took the form it did. The events of Jesus' life, or the way in which those events have entered language, exercise a kind of linguistic imperialism upon the language Paul uses about himself. Paul finds that the term fits his experience, that it has 'empirical fit' (Ramsey, passim).

5.1. Similarly, that Jesus was executed by crucifixion is a historical fact; that he was sacrified is not.

5.11. Paul sees synoptically the killing of an animal in a building and the execution of a criminal outside one. A singular event, the execution of Jesus, and a regular procedure, the killing of animals, are juxtaposed.

5.12. The event and the procedure are comparable as in each case life is lost and lost violently.

5.2. Why are animals killed in this way?

5.21. Men give one another presents; they eat meals together.

5.22. It is not unknown for a slice to be taken from an animal on the hoof, but more usually the animal is killed first. And there is a preference for the cooked over the raw. The animal is killed and cooked.

5.23. A present may be given to someone one likes; or one may wish to make up a quarrel.

5.24. If a man is reluctant to make up a quarrel himself, he may ask someome else to do it for him; or someone else might offer to do so of his own volition.

5.25. If the forensic analogue of 'all have sinned' (Rom.3:23) is 'all men are criminals', that is tantamount to saying that all men have a quarrel with God. It might be illiberal to add that God has a quarrel with men, but Paul does not shy away from illiberality. Or can a man love his enemy and quarrel with him at the same time?

5.26 Those who have made up a quarrel may be said to be at one.

5.3. Paul thinks that Jesus was appointed to make up the quarrel between God and man. He also thinks that those who have ceased to quarrel may share a common meal.

5.31. If an 'eristic' dispute is one in which I seek to gain a victory over the one with whom I am in disagreement and a 'dialectical' dispute is one where I seek to convert non-agreement into agreement (Collingwood, 1942, p.181), then it is more dialectical to lose the dispute than to win it.

5.32. Can what was in fact a dispute between Jesus of Nazareth on the one hand and Caiaphas and Pilate on the other be read in this way? And did the dispute occur because Jesus' theocratic views left no room or too little room for the way Pilate and Caiaphas were organizing religious and political affairs?

5.4. If it is the judge's function to condemn criminals, it is also his function to acquit the innocent. It is also his task to see that the victim of injustice is granted compensation. The granting of compensation may be complicated by the death of the victim.

5.41. Compensation in this case can still be granted, if the dead victim can be redescribed as alive and truly so described.

5.42. It is possible to imagine what is the opposite of the case and to imagine that what is the case only *seems* to be the case.

5.43. What is it that enables one to assert as true what one can imagine to be true?

5.5. If 'we may freely say that the bones of Jesus lie somewhere in Palestine' (Gregor Smith*, 1966, p.103), if the historian truly believes or rightly thinks that that statement is true, then the sense of saying that Jesus, after the conclusion of his historical life, is 'alive' is different from the sense of saying that he was 'alive' before it. The two senses are not univocal, but analogous. Or did Jesus' 'too, too sullied flesh' (*sic* Jenkins, 1982, p.129 and pp.436 ff) simply melt and resolidify? The word 'alive' in the second sense is borrowed from the empirical realm and lent to the theological.

5.51. Paul's use of the phrase 'spiritual body' (1 Cor.15) suggests that reflections of this kind (6.81.) are permissible, if not mandatory. A 'spiritual' body is as much as to say a metaphorical one, even if to say *only* that is not sufficient to explain one.

5.52. The temptation here to fill Paul's *lacunae* by supplying him with the synoptic and Johannine narratives is very strong. And it would be wrong to repel the boarders by claiming that Paul is devoid of synoptic and Johannine nonsense, for the nonsense is not the author's but the reader's. 'For the texts are a somewhat childish expression of very great faith, and they lose nothing by being the inconsistent, historically contestable expression of facts of which history has no knowledge' (Loisy, 1931, 2, p.239, my translation with the kind assistance of Mr. Clarke).

5.53. But it is true for all that that it is not Paul's style to tell stories.

5.6. Another favourite antithesis of Paul is 'flesh' and 'spirit'.

5.61. Broadly the one refers to human and the other to divine activity.

5.62. 'Spirit' can be used indifferently of either human or divine activity, but tends to mean the latter.

5.63. But 'flesh' has no theological use.

5.7. By 'flesh' Paul means that all men are mortal and bad; sometimes only the former.

---

* (1913-1968). He regarded footnotes as a sign of indiscipline.

5.71. Without giving such a fuller analysis of crime and guilt as Shakespeare offers in Macbeth, Paul sometimes lists some of the ways in which men are bad: for example, they are malicious and whisper (Rom.1:29). Or he gives a brief disquisition on prostitution (1 Cor.6:12 ff). Or he speaks about 'flesh' without being in any way specific: 'For those who live according to the flesh set their minds on the things of the flesh' (Rom.8:5).

5.8. What is 'spirit'?

5.81. 'Spirit' has its genesis in what the Stoics called 'air in motion'; in the lungs or outside them. Its absence is what makes a glass fail to mist over when held to the nostrils of a corpse.

5.82. We are warned, of course, against the genetic fallacy. When talking of 'spirit', it is only too easy to be either fallacious or vacuous.

5.83. Anyone who breathes is vital. Vitality is shown in power and intelligence.

5.84. Abnormal vitality is striking. Its lurid manifestation is enthusiasm, rightly described as 'a horrid thing, a very horrid thing' (Butler J. <1692-1752>, the last Bishop of Durham, in the eyes of 'the powers that be' <Rom.13:1, 2 Cor.4:18>, to be a theologian).

5.85. It is arguable that Paul shares this view. Paul is interested in the cybernesis of communities, in their organization and education, though he is not above introducing the part of the poet-intellectual (e.g. 1 Cor.12:28; cf 4.32.). Paul is interested in community spirit — there the word is out: the relation between pneumatology and ecclesiology in the Pauline epistles may be summed up as *esprit de corps*.

5.86. 'Spirit' is a model for divine activity (Ramsey, 1973, pp.1 ff). Community spirit is what is caused, in Paul's view, by that activity. The difficulty of the term 'spirit' arises because it seems to require a clear and distinct idea not only of what is modelled by the model, but of the model itself.

5.9. Among radical transitions are the transition from not-being to being, birth, and the transition from being to not-being, death. Paul almost ignores the first of these and says a good deal about the second; or rather he says a little about it often, for his speech is nothing if not condensed. Betz (1979, p.114) calls Paul's language 'formulaic' and speaks of his 'abbreviations'.

5.91. Paul almost ignores the first, birth. But he does tell us that he has been 'set apart' before he was 'born' and 'called' through God's 'grace' (Gal.1:15). He is, of course, not bringing to speech what has not been brought to speech. He is citing or alluding to or writing in the light of Isaiah (42:6; 49:1, 5 f) and Jeremiah (1:5) — and thus he shows us that it is in principle possible for a theologian to avoid doing any theology of his own at all, a principle more honoured in the observance than in the breach.

5.92. Birth here is not perhaps a metaphor. Paul is not saying that he was born into the Christian family. From the first, from his entry into the world, or perhaps a little before it, he feels he had a life's task set. The metaphor, if it is one, resides in the word 'called': the task set is not a task he had set himself. When he speaks, he has words that speak themselves in his mind. He has been summoned by a voice whose decibels are measureless to man.

5.93. Birth here is perhaps a metaphor. Paul is not so much the son of his parents as the son of his God. God has not 'set apart' merely, nor 'called' merely, but has engendered Paul, has visited Paul's mother 'amid a snow-shower of gold at dead of night' (Pindar, *Isthmians*, VII,5).

5.94. A superficial reading of the fabulation that surrounds the birth of Jesus might lead one to suppose that the statement, 'Jesus was the son of God', displaces the statement, 'Jesus was the son of Joseph', and replaces it with 'Jesus was the son of his mother'. But this is to read the texts as though they came from the files of a registry of births, deaths and marriages. Jones (1979, pp.213 f) recounts how a certain Madame Foussé, after she had returned from a shopping expedition to buy a loofah, noted that her maid had not put it in the bathroom, but found it on the dinner table, lightly steamed and served with a white sauce. These are instances of misconstruction.

5.95. Birth here is perhaps literal *and* metaphorical or, as Jowett roundly puts it (1855, vol.1, p.217), '(h)ere *aphorisas* (sc. 'set apart') has a double meaning: first a literal and physical one; secondly, that of which this is a figure, – a spiritual one' (by 'spiritual' Jowett means, I take it, 'metaphorical', when the metaphor in question occurs within theological discourse). The statements, 'Paul was the son of his parents' and 'Paul was the son of his God', can run in parallel without strain, neither displacing the other. We need not suppose that 'the birth-story that is told of Jesus, Augustus, Alexander, Plato, and every pharaoh of Egypt since, at latest, the beginning of the Fifth Dynasty' (Toynbee, 1956, p.280) should, when told of Paul, be taken *au pied de la lettre*.

6.1. But there is the 'birth' of the world, a cosmogony.

6.11. Or rather its 'fabrication'. *Homo faber* may speak of *deus faber*. The poetics, so to speak, of the artisan allow us to speak of the poetics of God, of 'theopoetics' (the word, at least, is Wilder's <1976>). There is an analogy between making a poem, a table and a world.

6.12. To make a world, to fabricate, when what is fabricated is a world, is like giving birth to a child. This is cosmogony (6.1.). Or, to explore the arabic cognate of the Hebrew *bara*, to 'create', it is like paring a reed for writing or fashioning an arrow for shooting: at time T-1 God fashioned an arrow, at time T1 he shot it; at time T-1 God pared a reed, at time T1 he began writing (6.11.). This is creation, sc. fabrication.

6.13. And he has not stopped.

6.14. But this is pure Montanism, sc. the view that God is alive and walks and talks.

6.15. Yes.

6.16. Or to make a world is like founding a city, like undertaking a colonial enterprise, thus calling 'into existence the things that do not exist' (Rom.4:17). Or it is like a big bang: at time T-1 God held a plunger, at time T1 he depressed it. Or there was a big bang *tout court*.

6.17. If 'creation' is already a metaphor, a metaphor from the lexical field of fabrication, when it is used of cosmogony (or of cosmology rather, for cosmogony is redolent of the congress of man with woman or of the results of that congress), it becomes a metaphor at a remove, when Paul speaks of his entry into the Christian movement as 'creation' or as 'new creation': 'if any one is in Christ he is a new creation' (2 Cor.5:17). God fabricates Christians, as he once fabricated a world.

6.18. There are worlds and worlds. To cross the threshold, the *limen*, of a lawyer's office is to enter a different world, where the talk is of 'collateral estoppel' and 'negligence *per se*' (Ross' examples, 1981, p.166). To enter the Lamb or the Elephant is to enter a world 'where, as we know, they stop whimpering with another bitter and so far from sneering at all things, hang pictures of winners at Kempton and stars of the 'nineties'. Something good we have for each other is freed there, and in some degree and for a while the miasma of time is rolled back without obliging us to deny the present' (Wisdom, 1953, p.167). When Paul joined the Christian movement, he, too, entered a world, where they talked of justice and the awakening of Jesus from sleep. But Paul's new world was not a specialist world, but cosmic in scope, a world world-wide.

6.19. To use the vocabulary of Jew and Christian, which arguably is later than Paul's day and systematically distorts what he thinks he was doing, for he was becoming not a Christian but a Jew *par excellence*, Paul was a Jew, changed his mind and became a

Christian. Physiologically speaking, he became a 'limb' of that 'body'. He became the 'hand' that held the 'hammer' that beat the Judaisers?

6.2.   Paul was a Jew for Jews, changed his mind and became a Jew for Jews and non-Jews.

6.21.   If Paul was 'called', he was also 'sent'. Paul, in Paul's view at least, was an 'apostle'.

6.22.   Paul was not 'sent' or not now 'sent' by Caiaphas (Ac.9:1) to discipline a group that was heterodox. He was sent by God to discipline a group that was heterodox. The subject of the verb 'to send' is God.

6.23.   'Unless we are either very unsophisticated or very sophisticated, passages in the Bible which use the word 'God' are hazardous in the extreme: for they read as if God has been observed to say and to do precisely what is there described ...' (Ramsey, 1973a, p.31).

6.24.   Persons who are sent by other persons, even in the case where the other person is God, are sent for some purpose. What purpose did God formulate in God's mind or what purpose formulated itself in Paul's mind?

6.25.   What did it now occur to Paul to do? What was it that urgently impressed itself on Paul's mind? What was the task he set himself or that he thought he had been set?

6.26.   An 'apostle' is someone whose task is to speak about God and about Jesus; and, on occasion (or, for Paul, on many occasions), about himself. And what he was to speak was to be spoken to everybody; or to anybody who would listen. And that involved going abroad, travelling.

6.27.   An 'apostle' is a travelling speaker.

6.28.   If Jesus in the Fourth Gospel 'reveals', in Bultmann's phrase (1955, Vol.II, p.66) 'nothing but that he is the Revealer', he is not revealing very much. He has failed to let the cat out of the bag.

6.29.   Paul's assertion that God has 'sent' him , his use of the sending model, is an infertile assertion of the same kind. The assertion on its own is merely formal or vacuous. What we want to know is something of the character and purposes and activity of the sovereign or sovereigns, president or presidents or president and vice-president, whose agent or envoy Paul is.

6.3.   If Paul is convinced, if it has occurred to Paul and Paul now rests convinced that he is to speak about God and Jesus, or if he is convinced that he is within hearing distance of God's lips, teeth and tongue, what within that distance has he heard?

6.31. If Paul uses the 'communication' model, if he uses of God the word 'word' or of God's words the word 'words', *what* is it that has been communicated to him? *What* has the 'enskied' (3.82.) Stentor (5.92.) said?

6.32. Or, prescinding from the assumption that the envoy Paul is accurately carrying out the instructions of his sovereign, we may ask, *athletically*, what race Paul is running or which of his punches is reaching the target, or, *militarily*, what victorious campaign this soldier is celebrating or in what campaign this prisoner was taken.

6.33. We may ask, but we need not answer.

6.34. Or shall we say that it is Paul's purpose to talk about God and Jesus and that that is his purpose, because Jesus paradigmatically instantiates benevolence and that in doing so Jesus is backed up by God?

6.35. One answer, perhaps *any* answer, is better than none, though *that* answer, the 'paradigmatic instantiation ...', may be judged worse than some. But let it stand for the moment.

6.4. Paul's imagination is anthropomorphic.

6.41. A man can hardly do otherwise.

6.42 Gone is the vigorous anthropomorphism of Homer's gods, the antics, unedifying perhaps, of Zeus and Hera. Is it not a matter for shame, writes Tertullian (*Ad Nationes*, II. 7 (7), 107, 5 f ⟨Miss. Imrie kindly located this reference for me⟩), *'tales deos credi quales homines non esse debeant'*, 'that the gods should be believed to be such as men ought not to be'. Anthropomorphism in theology demands moral criteria.

6.43. Gone is the anthropomorphism of the Old Testament. 'He has poured me out like milk and curdled me like cheese' (Job 10:10) is a palmary example and builds, on a sexual base, an infinite dairy person; dairying is denoted, a sequence of sexual events is connoted (in the womb the baby Job began to take shape).

6.44. And for God's 'nostril', distended in anger, we have 'anger'. The word ' 'aph' (Hebrew) that once meant both 'nostril' and 'anger' now means 'anger' alone. 'Like a vapour trail' (Templeton E.A., 'On Undoing the Past' ⟨unpublished paper⟩) the word's past is dispersed.

6.45. There is a dilution in concretion. We speak, says Wittgenstein (1978, p.71), of God's eye, but not of his eyebrow.

6.46. Why not?

6.47. The lips, teeth and tongue of the Godhead's Godmouth have been reduced to his 'word'. The Cheshire cat has its smile, but nothing to smile it with.

6.5. All the theologian needs to do, in order to construct a theology, is to construct an anthropology, but not too comprehensively, and then give capital letters to the terms used in the construction: for 'spirit' read 'Spirit'; for 'word' 'Word'.

6.51. What semantic shift is effected by an enlargement of letters?

6.52. You point out, of course, that the terms are asymptotic; that words that begin with large letters (and what large letters!) are not identical in meaning with words that begin with minuscules. We know, but not as we are known. The mirror imperfectly reflects (1 Cor.13:12).

6.53. But what a man sees when he looks in a mirror is himself.

6.54. True, but that is not to the point. What is to the point is that when a man looks into a pre-industrial or pre-post-modernist mirror, he will see himself only imperfectly. Similarly, if God (which God forbid!) were to read either pre-industrial or post-modernist theology, he would obtain only an imperfect conception of himself (unless, of course, he simply had better things to do). And if a man were to look over God's shoulder, if God were looking into a mirror, he would see imperfectly reproduced both God and himself. Similarly, when a man either reads theology or writes it.

6.55. But maybe Paul means (1 Cor.13:12) not that the mirror reflects imperfectly (for is not the mirror Corinthian? <Davidson, 1952, p.180, No.1309>), but that all mirrors show images of realities, but not realities.

6.6. But if the theologian does not have everything, he may have enough.

6.61. If the vigorous anthropomorphism, the anthropomorphism of the creative poet, the 'makar' (Scots), has left only vestiges, the hunter should be able not only to reconstruct in his imagination the animal whose tracks he can see, he should also be able to track it down and shoot it. The iceberg of Paul's imagery is, if also protuberantly anfractuous, largely submarine.

6.62. 'Yet before I had dreamed / That the rain water streamed / From Zeus and his chamber-pot sieve' (Aristophanes, Clouds, 373). Paul has less in common with Rabelais; Paul's language on the 'kingdom' is more restrained, more reduced, more spare. When Paul speaks of 'kingdom', as he rarely does, for he is no epigone content to repeat his master's voice, we should be able to find the king, the throne on which he sits and the subjects prostrate at his feet. The king has allies. He made a treaty once. He can do so again and improve the clauses: 'old covenant' is replaced by 'new' (2 Cor.3). Perhaps he can remove the clauses or retain enough to apply to himself only.

6.63. Political, monarchical imagery is vestigial in Paul, but not absent. Paul contracts, as it were, his stories to a single term; like the inmates of the asylum, whose stories were so well known to one another that for the stories they substituted numbers. The new arrival, we remember, who called a number and was greeted by no laughter, was told he did not tell the story well. If Paul's jokes are to be understood, the exegete must find the tale behind the number.

6.64. Not only does the king have his subjects, he has his vice-gerent.

6.65. And his conquering army that rases defences, that 'destroy(s) strongholds' (2 Cor.10:3 ff).

6.66. And the 'tenor' of Paul's 'vehicle' (4.97.) is that Paul is an effective speaker, on paper: 'his letters are weighty and strong, but ... his speech of no account' (2 Cor.10:10).

6.7. If the effect of Paul's letters is to floor his readers, what is the cause of the effect? What is the *content* of what he says?

6.71. It is not, as Bultmann claims for John, that 'Jesus reveals that he is the revealer' (6.28.).

6.72. If Paul has authority to say what he says (and he believes that he does), what is it he says that has this authority? What is he saying that he has not dreamt up, that has been dreamt up for him?

6.73. He is not merely saying that those who contradict him are wrong. He is saying something that is contradicted.

6.74. Which is easier, to say what is said to contradict Paul or what Paul says to contradict those contradictions?

6.8. Death, says Paul, contradicts life; and there are things less than death, but also less than life, that obstruct life, if they do not contradict it: rules and regulations, say, or self-congratulation and its obverse, self-doubt; what the translations call 'law' and 'boasting'. And self-congratulation and self-doubt are positive and negative modes of introspection.

6.81. Death, in Paul, means both *literally* the extinction of life and *metaphorically* the threat of extinction; both the cancellation of *esse* and the compromising of *bene esse*.

6.82. To say that 'death contradicts life' is to make 'death' the subject of a sentence. In what sense can it be so?

6.83. Death is a process that belongs to animal biology. As 'the last enemy' (1 Cor.15:26) it belongs to Canaanite mythology (Gibson, 1979, p.167).

6.84. Which is tantamount to saying that it belongs to the figure of speech called 'personification'.

6.85. Which is a sub-species of metaphor: it 'requires metaphor' (Ross, 1981, p.151).

6.86. Bultmann differs from Heidegger in that for 'nothing' Bultmann puts 'God' and for 'death' 'Christ' (Körner, 1957, p.71). Paul's imagery is Bultmann's twin. Paul differs from Heidegger in the same way.

6.87. It is clear that for Paul 'death' is not a terminal category, that regulations may have relative value, if any, and introspection none.

6.88. But to speak of 'life' and 'death' is not to speak non-exhaustively. The terms are very broad. It should be possible to speak at a level of lesser abstraction.

6.9. The first pope adopts at Antioch a racist position, even if to say that Peter maintains that the Jews are the *Herrenvolk* would be to confuse a runaway pig with a charging rhinoceros. What Peter says or what we can infer he said (Gal.2:15) is that we 'are Jews by birth and not Gentile *sinners*' (italics are mine, not Peter's).

6.91. By straining, constraining the familial metaphor to theological use, Paul counters by saying that God is the 'father' of *all* men, not *some* men.

6.92. The restraints of the context within which Paul is imagining do not allow him to add that God is the 'mother' of all women. The observation is pertinent in what after all is a *Laywoman's Guide*.

6.93. 'Damn braces. Bless relaxes' (Blake, *Proverbs of Hell*). Our context is blest with unbraced relaxes. We can add it for him.

6.94. Whether all men and all women accept this position is not to the point. Something can be the case whether or not it is known to be the case or granted to be the case.

6.95. The notion can be completed by the assertion that God is the 'mother *and* father' of all men and women, but the point needs neither sharpening by the writer nor acumen in the reader. We are dealing not with a rapier, but with a 'dull thud': 'How did that strike you?' it is asked in *The Lady's Not For Burning*. 'With a dull thud, Tyson. With a dull thud' is the reply.

6.96. If racism is given a legal backing, it is law that must go.

6.97. And, one might add, if 'angels' give the law their backing, 'angels' must go, together with the law (Gal.3:19 claims that 'angels' are responsible, or are *in part* responsible, for the law, for the law is 'administered by angels'). And Moses goes too. If there is a relation between God and man and if that relation can be modelled as a relation in which we are to imagine the passage of communication, then the word 'angels' here indicates that while communication may have been correctly made it may not have been correctly received. *Something* seems to have gone wrong between God and the 'angels' and something *more* between the 'angels' and men; and women, more like, for 'when the *woman* saw that the tree was good for food ...' (Gen.3:6).

7.1. 'Angels' belong to the communications theory of the ancient Near East. It is sufficient to hold, indeed Paul implies that it is sufficient for *him* to hold, that messages are sent by a messenger, not by messengers, by God in the singular and not by 'angels' in the plural. There is not a group that has to be 'sent down the sky', after having first been 'tired with talking', as the sun by Heracleitus and his friend (Callimachus, *Ep.2*, trans. Cory W.J.). Indeed, no messenger is required at all. 'Enskied Stentor' can be heard from where he is, being who he is, or he who is, or, according to the conventions of theological orthography, He Who Is. The messengers are otiose.

7.11. You can multiply entities beyond necessity and you can multiply one by one; a senior wrangler is not required: '... an intermediary implies more than one; but God is one' (Gal.3:20) — who knows what Paul or one of his glossators is saying here? Galatians, we have it on Browning's authority, provides us with 'twenty-nine distinct damnations' in one of its verses; for this verse (3:20) the commentators provide us with four hundred and thirty distinct interpretations, though Schlier (1971, p.161, fn.2) thinks that this number depends less on the accuracy of the calculation and more on the time that is said to have elapsed between 'covenant' and 'law' (Gal.3:17). This particular figure, 430, is the calculation of Benjamin Jowett (1855, p.268).

7.12. Whether, of course, those who speak of 'angels' are multiplying *beyond* necessity, or substracting *below* it, is not a question that Paul himself entertains. All he asserts or may be taken to be asserting is that if 'angels' are real entities, there is an entity *more* real; or that there is that than which nothing provides more accurate communication.

7.13. If law is dropped and Moses with the law, that leaves Jesus in a palmary position. The lawgiver is not the highest kind of animal. 2 Cor.3 makes this claim: law is a 'dispensation of death, carved in letters on stone'; splendid, certainly, but Moses cannot hold up a candle to Jesus.

7.2. Who is Jesus?

7.21. If we can ask what Paul was 'sent' to do, we can ask what Jesus was 'anointed' to do. Or if the notion of 'anointing' can be regarded as recessive (Vermes, 1973, pp.158 f), we can ask what Jesus was 'appointed' to do. And the shift, from 'anoint' to 'appoint' is not a shift from imagery, but within it. 'Appoint' is less olfactory than 'anoint', but not less pictorial, unless it is true to say that a Mondrian is less pictorial than a Rubens. Is not the relating of God to Jesus via the model of enlightened preferment quite colourful in its way?

7.22. If a lawgiver is what Jesus was not, despite the contrary, if implicit, claim that Matthew makes, what was he? For in the Sermon on the Mount, 'that collection of sayings by an unknown author, representing what he believed to be the teaching of Jesus' (Gregor Smith, *obiter dictum*), the speaker within the narrative retains his jots and tittles, a most unlikely thing for the speaker outside the narrative to have done. What was he? What did Paul imagine Jesus was? If Jesus' views were illuminating, what light for whom was thrown on what? What makes 'good' the news that Jesus gave? What value or values did he oppose to the value of the law? What was it of his that made the law less valuable or of no value at all?

7.23. Paul speaks of the 'light that has shone in darkness', that has 'shone in our hearts', 'in the face of Jesus Christ' (2 Cor.4:6). The symbolism is common and has been studied (Bultmann, 1967, pp.323 ff). God has shed light on Jesus and Jesus has shed light on Paul. But it is easier to explain the symbolism than to explain why it has been used.

7.3. The idea of 'deconstruction' is abroad (this is very nearly literally true) and it may perhaps help us to reformulate the problem. People speak or write with the intention of talking sense; not always, of course, but often enough. In terms of the 'wisdom' and 'folly' models of 1 Cor.1-3, people, in Paul's view, succeed in talking nonsense. What appears to them to be sense is nonsense and nonsense sense. Paul's theological views, that is, 'deconstruct' the theology of the Corinthians. At the same time Paul, or God, for that matter, goes on talking. What about?

7.31. The Corinthian system of thought, like the Jewish legal system, has its limits. What system or what other thing does Paul oppose to it?

7.4. 'The word of the cross' (1 Cor.1.18).

7.41. If Paul is telling us that a criminal was executed, we want to know what crimes had been committed. Paul does not tell us.

7.42. Paul may be telling us that if you take the larger view Jesus was innocent and that that larger view calls into question the narrower view that made Jesus a criminal.

7.43. And he might just mean that there is an analogy between the narrow jurisprudence that put Jesus to death and the philosophy in Corinth (Senft *obiter dictum*). The Corinthian philosophy, whatever it is, is a narrow philosophy. What is Paul's broader philosophy?

7.44. In Paul's part of Corinth there are not many philosophers (1 Cor.1:26 'not many of you are wise'). The Corinthians are just quarrelling maybe, while Paul believes in maintaining agreement or reaching it.

7.45. Maybe Paul means that in so far as there are any philosophers in Corinth they should learn to be indifferent to their philosophy (cf. Braun, 1962, pp.159 ff). Paul's philosophy permits him to be indifferent to any philosophy or to be a philosopher 'as if' (1 Cor.7:29 ff) one were not.

7.5. People die; and Jesus did. But 'death' can also be a strong metaphor. As authors know, a man reading can be 'dead to the world'; as readers know, a man writing 'dead from the neck up'.

7.51. Or a man may be indifferent to the world, or to a philosophy, may not *reck* of it.

7.6. Jesus took on the Jewish legal system and had a bad time as a result. Paul is having a bad time with the Corinthians. He is perhaps, too, encouraging them to take on board the problems offered to them by their environment: where, for example, are they to buy meat?

7.61. Under the guise, as it were, of talking about the death of Jesus, Paul is *really* talking or is talking *pari passu* about the death of himself and his correspondents.

7.62. If we remove the metaphor, Paul is talking about his own indifference and recommending it to others.

7.63. If we keep the metaphor, it can apply not only to Paul in Corinth, but to Jesus before Golgotha: Jesus was dead before he died; if we remove it, he was indifferent, he '*cared* not for it', he did not 'mind' it (cf. 1 Cor.7:21). Both the metaphor 'death' and its translation 'indifference' can be extrapolated backwards, can extend backwards into the life of Jesus.

7.64. Does it also extend forwards to suggest that Paul will literally die? Does the metaphor carry with it the suggestion of Paul's literal death?

7.7. If so, then the lacuna that follows his literal death can be filled with the metaphor 'life', the condition of being 'alive', and the metaphor 'resurrection', the process of coming to 'life'.

7.71. All he need then do is to suppose that the fiction that redescribes death as 'life' is truly so describing it.

7.8. That there is an Archimedean, a philosophical point outside a philosophy that allows a lever to be exerted on that philosophy is simply presupposed by Paul. His presupposition works in practice well enough for him. Paul is indifferent, he is a free man. For having a philosophy with a point outside it allows him to be indifferent to and free from philosophies that are either ignorant of such a point or are in error as to its nature.

7.81. The point is a formal one: that Paul's philosophy allows him to be free from a philosophy; in this case the Corinthian one or a Corinthian one or some Corinthian ones.

7.82. But what Corinthian philosophy or philosophies?

7.83. It is very difficult reliably to give content to what the Corinthians were thinking, though this difficulty has hardly been sufficient to deter scholarship from solving it.

7.84. In various ways.

7.9. 'All he need then do ...' (7.71.)? ''All' ...? Did you say, 'All'?', Macduff asks (Macbeth, IV, iii, 217) and it may be asked with him. For it is less of a fiction surely, the cynic would insist, to redescribe life as 'death' than death as 'life'.

7.91. 'Resurrection' occupies one point in a system of co-ordinates; belongs to a symbolic complex. If it is withdrawn from the futurological (2.4.) context in which Paul includes it and is transferred elsewhere, can it survive there?

7.92. Paul's Greek for 'resurrection' offers him two linguistic possibilities: 'awakening from sleep' and 'becoming erect after being recumbent', homo erectus for homo supinus. Neither of these much helps us here.

7.93. If there are two ways of saying what Jesus then did (or, if you must, what was then done to him): (1) he 'awoke', (2) he 'stood up', there is one way of saying, but three ways of meaning, how what he then did was apprehended: he 'appeared', sc. he was 'seen' (1 Cor.15:5): the semantic field of 'seeing' Jesus covers (1) physical, (2) imaginative, and (3) intellectual apprehension; the interpreter, that is, is offered these three, promiscuous options.

7.94. The clarity with which Paul denies that philosophy can set a limit here, sc. 'death is not the end of life', is not then matched by the clarity with which he explains his alternative, sc. 'death is a liminal caregory'.

8.1. In writing of Jesus' death, Paul not only considers also his correspondents' death and his own; he means also the 'death' of Jesus' executioners.

8.11. It is the society that disposed of Jesus that is itself disposed of; Judaism, not Jesus, that is called in question.

8.12. The opposing view is that a society may dispose of its law-breakers.

8.13. And if the society is such that the presiding place in its linguistic system is occupied by the word 'God', that society will suppose that *its* rejection of its lawbreakers is joined by *God's* rejection. The technical term for God's rejection is 'curse': 'He who is hanged is cursed by God' (Dt.21:23).

8.14 So much the worse for God, Paul might have rejoined. And so he almost does, except that between the Lawgiver (God) and the lawgiver (Moses) he intercalates a 'flight' of law-carriers (the 'angels' of Gal.3:19 that 'sing' Judaism 'to its rest' <Hamlet, V, 365>).

8.15. Thus theology is saved by claiming, so to speak, that the socket was not at fault, but the connection; that Moses and the angels could between them only offer a current that alternated between just and unjust, while the Sermon on the Mount, once Matthew's contribution has been removed, and Paul's analogue, Paul's account of God's justice, once Paul's contribution (*contra* Paul) has been removed (the non-universalist elements, say; the elements that suggest that one day God will delete or will have deleted his enemies), are the result of a direct and well-connected current. And this may explain why Israel was so often in revolt.

8.16. With a little expense of energy, the model of electrical power may be brought into relation with Paul's 'light' symbolism in 2 Cor.3. Jesus, Paul claims, was a luminary of greater brilliance than Moses. God supplies the power; Jesus glows.

8.2. A judge or judges, then, applied the law or laws to Jesus' case and found him guilty.

8.21. The spectator who 'judges' Jesus innocent finds the judges guilty or the law unjust, or not applied, or misapplied.

8.3. The problem with the laws is that they may not be very good.

8.31. Where they are good or good enough, it may not at any point be clear how they are to be applied.

8.32. But law can give a society structure. A lawgiver can throw light on a society, can guide it prudently.

8.33. But there may be other means that can shed more light, some notion more elastic than law such as morality.

8.34. It is not, Collingwood (1942, pp.111 ff) might say, a regularian morality that is required, but one that is de-ontological; a transition, he might add (1939, p.106), from 'the second-grade morality of custom and precept'.

8.35. Is morality, be it de-ontological, the 'gospel' that replaces law?

8.4. The 'good news' that Jesus brought (Braun, 1962, pp.283 ff) can be bifurcated into a 'you may' and a 'you ought'. Braun's brevity is not at fault.

8.41. In Paul's view 'you may' takes priority.

8.42. If morality is the category we need, it is God's morality that is primarily in question.

8.43. The question arises whether when the word 'morality' is used in theology it so changes its meaning that some other word is required. For 'all words become new, when they are transposed from their own location to a different one' (*omnia vocabula fiunt nova, quando e suo foro in alienum transferuntur:* Luther, *Weimarer Ausgabe*, 39,1; 231,1-3 <Disp.1537>). Is the word 'morality' here making the kind of transition that compels Paul to speak not of 'wisdom', but of 'folly' (1 Cor.1 ff)? Does 'morality' here mean 'immorality'?

8.44. Dialectically (it is said; confusedly, it might be added), Paul speaks both of God's 'folly' and his 'wisdom'.

8.45. By this argument, or by parity of practice 'morality' may be used in theology provided that we are confident that we may not be meaning the right thing by it, but may even be meaning by it the opposite of the right thing.

8.5. 'Philosophy is not what you thought', Paul is telling us. 'Philosophy is what *I* think'.

8.6. The function of the word 'God' in Pauline theology is to relativise any context, but there is no other access to what relativises a context than a relative one. What appears to be a philosophy may be an inadequate one; what appears to be legal may be the reverse of legality. Is it only an appearance that it is the position of his opponents that appears to Paul to require adjustment and not his own?

8.61. If this is indeed the function of the word 'God', the word allows Paul to transcend the context in which he is. He is extricably implicated; inextricability is only an appearance.

8.62. Paul's theological point should enable him to take his own theology *cum grano salis* (and nothing need dissuade us from taking our own in the same way).

8.63. Nor is there anything in Paul's writing that can persuade us that Paul did what his theological point should have enabled him to do.

8.64. But is that fair? He does after all concede that 'we see in a mirror dimly' (1 Cor.13:12), that we are dealing with reflections, not with realities.

8.65. The point at any rate allows freedom of movement.

8.66. If morality is a viable category, with the qualification introduced at 8.45., the criteria for knowing how to move, when you are free to move, are moral. Three of Paul's words, if we remember the weakness of the ancient world for triadic formulae, are 'faith, hope and love' and 'the greatest of these', for Paul, was 'love' (and, for Brahms, Clara Schumann) (1 Cor.13:13).

8.7. Paul's criteria are criteria that *occur* to him. They do not need to be *excogitated* by him.

8.71. Nor are they merely theoretical. They are not only criteria that *might* have been applied, but criteria that *were* applied. They have practical and paradigmatic instantiation, as well as in his own, in the career of Jesus.

8.72. Admittedly when Jesus' career has been reduced to a mathematical point.

8.73. The word 'death', in its literal and metaphorical senses, is how Paul explicates Jesus' career negatively. Paul's brevity, like Braun's (8.4.), is not at fault.

8.74. But what is often called a *theologia crucis*, a 'theology of the cross', and might be called a *theologia mortis*, a 'theology of death', has a *theologia vitae*, a 'theology of life', as its counterpart. Paul's antitheses are not at fault either.

8.75. It would be wrong to ignore this counterpart, this 'theology of life'. Neither Jesus nor Paul was guilty of a *Thanatostrieb*, a 'death-instinct'. It is a short-circuit to say that Jesus came to die.

8.76. He did nothing of the kind. Is an inevitable consequence necessarily a purpose? It is all too easy to make, as it were, a synizesis, a crasis, a conflation, a confusion of a purpose and a consequence. Where Paul's Greek is too often ambiguous, Paul's interpreters are too often masochistic.

8.8. In 1 Cor.13:13 Paul resorts to, or conventionally relapses into, a triadic formula: 'faith, hope, love abide'. Let us consider 'faith' alone.

8.81. At the beginning of the Christian movement the word became a best-seller; like the archaeopteryx and to the archaeopteryx's surprise, it *took off*.

8.82. The semantic field of 'faith' is the inter-personal: a man who is trustworthy may be trusted.

8.83. Its use in theology ineluctably involves anthropomorphism.

8.84. 'Faith' allows Paul to concentrate not on what *he* does, but on what *God* does. It is a model by which Paul examines God, not himself. It has implications for Paul himself, but these implications are not for Paul's own eyes.

8.85. By opposing 'faith' and 'works' Paul is opposing God's works and his own. He is opposing two activities. To speak of 'God's activity' is to use an anthropomorphic model. That is what Paul was doing, whether or not he thought he was doing it.

8.86. God's activity is what is responded to and 'faith' is the response.

8.87. On the assumption that something is modelled by the model, certain consequences are likely to follow: Paul travelled in great measure and wrote in some measure. Broadly speaking, the Christian movement expanded. Paul makes the claim that these historical facts can be correlated with his symbolic system; further, that there are 'facts', but 'facts' which are not of a historical kind, that are symbolised by his system. The analyst of Paul's system may either make or not make the same claim.

8.88. We do not have 'God's history with man' (contra Gregor Smith, 1966, p.21), but 'God's 'history' with man'. The word 'history' in theology, where the gesta, the 'things done', are gesta dei, 'things done by God', is used not univocally, but analogically.

8.9. 'In the beginning is relation' (Buber, 1937, p.18), as for Bertie Wooster his Great Aunt Julia, though a greater Great Aunt, Dahlia, can be thought (Wodehouse P.G., the Blandings novels, passim).

8.91. 'Faith' means relation, but a qualified relation, a relation of a certain sort. It is a relation of confidence.

8.92. With what is the relation?

8.93. With everything.

8.94. With God and with everything else.

8.95. The relation is supported by positive features of the world and may persist despite negative features.

8.96. Brooke in The Great Lover lists some positive features: '... the rough male kiss of blankets; grainy wood; live hair that is shining and free; blue-massing clouds; the keen unpassioned beauty of a great machine ...'. And Sophocles some negative ones: ' ... envy, factions, strife, battles and slaughters; and last of all ... age dispraised, infirm, unsociable, unfriended, with whom all woe of woe abides' (Oedipus Coloneus 1234 ff). In Rom.4:19, Abraham, in the story, could have cited old age and Sarah the menopause. (The conclusion of the story is, of course, absurd, but the author of it does not need us to tell him that. Though the author of the story does not tell us what logic he is using, it is arguable that he knew what it was. The author is not to blame if we mislocate the genre he is using. His point is

clear enough: good results always follow, even if they have to
be postponed. And they do not always have to be postponed.)

9.1. One of the correlates of this kind of confidence is God's 'promise'.

9.11. The noun, 'God', in the genitive is important. A man's word is
not always as good as his bond. I refrain from providing examples. But God's 'word' is. When God says 'I will do', he does.

9.12. God's assertion (or 'assertion', if you will <for to the most real
entity we are attributing unreal teeth>) that he will act has the
unfortunate implication that he is not acting, but the fortunate
implication that he will. Though if he is not yet doing A, he
may be doing B. But anyway, Paul now thinks, God *is* doing A.
He is not *promising* to do; he is *doing*; he is doing now what he
once promised to do.

9.2. Another correlate of man's confidence is God's 'grace'. One of
the relata in the relation is qualified by, is characterised by,
confidence; the other by 'grace'.

9.21. It would be symmetrical to suppose that if man is confident in
God, God is confident in man. Paul probably supposes that man
does not inspire confidence, even, perhaps especially, in God.
Might it not in any case be a little blasphemous to suppose God
to be inspired? Whatever the reason, Paul's correlate is 'grace';
the correlate of Paul's faith in God is not God's 'faith' in Paul,
but God's 'grace' given to Paul.

9.22. 'Grace' is the name for a relation where symmetry, possible
where the Graces are Three, is impossible.

9.23. 'Grace' implies that a forensic description of God's relation
with man is instable.

9.24. The semantic field of 'grace' (again) is the inter-personal. The
field has been classically described by Oman (1917; to which
might be added Paton, 1955, pp.337 ff). 'Grace' is an inter-personal term, whose inter-personal correlate is 'faith'. The relations between judge and criminal, between king and subject,
between general and soldier are secondary relations. Such relations as that between father and son, brother and brother,
friend and friend are the primary ones.

9.25. But if the relation between God and man is to be fully described, 'multi-model discourse' (Ramsey, *passim*) will be required. A father is *id quo maius cogitari possit*, that than which
a greater (a king, say) can be thought, for a king's authority
and power exceeds a father's, and a judge may show greater
penetration than a father where the criminality of a son is in

question. But neither king nor judge may be in possession of a father's 'entrails' (Phil.2:1 <RSV: 'affection'>). Where kings or judges have them, they may be professionally bound to ignore them.

9.26. The inter-personal is Paul's primary language.

9.3. But the weight 'grace' bears is a function of the whole context in which it occurs. In that context, 'grace' sums up briefly, for it is only one word, what Jesus did and what God did when Jesus did it; what God did as an indirect and Jesus as a direct agent. And not only that, but it sums up too what both of these *are* doing and what it is expected that they *will* do. If a verb in theology has one tense, the other tenses are not far away.

9.31. And it is not *mere* action that is summarised, but *qualified* action. 'Grace' tells us not only *that* Jesus acted, but *how* he acted. His is the good activity of a good father or a good friend. It is action that is analogous to the giving of gifts.

9.32. But the connotations are not only sweet, but *glukupikros*, 'bitter-sweet', for purchase means outlay and the receiver is impelled in his turn to become himself a purchaser.

9.33. If the whole context is involved, not only the disposition and activity of the givers are in question. Who are the receivers, we must ask, and how do they receive? How did they at time T1 and how do they at time T2?

9.34. Let time T1 be the Palestinian career of Jesus. In terms of the imagery of the giving of gifts, to say that Jesus' Palestinian career was terminated by execution is as much as to say that the gifts were turned down. The matter becomes more serious if the gifts that Jesus bore were gifts that he was given to bear, if behind the direct agent, Jesus, there stands an indirect agent, God.

9.35. But the language of the giving of gifts is odd, for one is thinking less of the giving of gifts than of the giving of oneself.

9.4. The 'gift', let us say, is companionship; the companionship of a father with his sons or a brother with his brothers.

9.41. Let time T2 be our own time. It is arguable that there is an analogy between time T2 and time T1. And time T1 is a paradigm case. For time T2 time T1 is heuristic.

9.42. If between these times we interpolate Paul's time, it is not difficult to see why Paul saw that language appropriate for time T1, was analogously appropriate for his own time, why he can say of himself that, for example, he has been 'crucified' (Gal. 2:19) or that he 'bears in his body the dying of Jesus' (2 Cor. 4:10). But it should not be impossible to put oneself on the other side of the equation, with the executioners and not with the executed: I am not one killed, but a killer.

9.43. If the relata are God and man and the relata can be modelled familially as 'father' and 'son' or 'sons', grace accurately describes the relation.

9.44. 'Love' is a synonym of 'grace' and can replace it without addition or loss.

9.45. But the relation is not being thought of symmetrically, the relation has a direction: from God to man.

9.46. Rubbish. It is both more confused and better than that.

9.47. 'Grace' can as well describe the disposition as the acts that proceed from the disposition.

9.48. To give Jonas' views (1971) explicit relational or inter-personal form, we might say that 'grace' is God's conscious involvement to ensure that man is consciously involved, with the further implication that man's conscious involvement should not be frustrated. Jonas' Latin would then run: *velle me velle te velle te velle*, 'I willingly will that you willingly will', when God is understood as the subject of the first and man of the second pair of verbs. Aristotle's phrase, 'all men by nature desire to know', might then be given theological specification: 'all men by nature desire to know God', that is, it is God's nature to ensure that man's nature should be of this kind.

9.49. But this is not to deny that there are other good things than God that may rightly be desired. While Aristotle's phrase may be given *theological* specification, it may also be specified in other ways. The Song of Solomon, for example, can as well be given a secular as a theological reading. There are, that is, objects of knowledge other than God; there are girl-friends and boy-friends quite apart from the God-friend: all men by nature desire to know their girl-friends and boy-friends.

9.5. 'Grace' is one of a number of Paul's terms that seem to give us 'the gospel *in nuce*'. The statement is worthless, if we are not prepared to call in either the nuthatch or the nutcracker; if we are not prepared to state what we think 'the gospel' is. Each of the words for which this claim is made must be examined with care. While some of this number possess synonyms or virtual synonyms, 'love' and 'grace' for example, it will often be found that a different perspective on 'the gospel' is being offered. Those differences merit consideration.

9.6. Jesus of Nazareth founded the Christian movement. Whether or not he intended to do so, he was taken to have done so.

9.61. Black (1979, p.26) uses or entertains the use of a volcanic metaphor to describe the vitality of metaphors: metaphors are 'active', 'dormant' or 'extinct'.

9.62. Paul became a *member* of the Christian movement. The metaphor in 'member' may be revitalised or re-awakened by saying that he became a member of that *body*; much as Hamlet revitalises or re-awakens the dormant metaphor of 'sleep' for death by adding 'perchance to dream' (Proudfoot, *obiter dictum*); or we could say, less arthritically, that Paul became not a 'member' of the Christian 'body', but the calamus- or pen-holding or paper-folding and envelope-inserting hand of the *corpus christianum*. And the metaphor may again be devitalized by saying that Paul became a member of a public body, or corporation.

9.63. Paul exercised a function within a group within which diverse functions were being exercised.

9.64 Jesus of Nazareth had outlined a symbolic system and a scheme of behaviour appropriate to that system (Geertz, 1968, pp.1 ff).

9.65. Paul is not so much concerned to repeat that system, though his familial symbols overlap with those of Jesus, as to evaluate it and apply his own new system to the circumstances of his time. Jesus' system, in Paul's estimation, sheds more light on the human condition and on the divine condition than Moses'; hence the relation of Jews to other peoples needs to be re-thought.

9.66. Paul stresses that he is not himself the founder, that he has not given the movement its shape. He is playing a subordinate role: 'Was Paul crucified for you?' he asks the Corinthians (1 Cor. 1:13). Paul did not start the movement; he belongs to it. In one of the social terminologies of his day, he belongs to the manager of the movement as a slave belongs to his slave-master.

9.7. We can devise theories of interpretation. Such theories can be proved useful only if they can be shown to be capable, when applied, of interpreting texts.

9.71. It can of course be asserted that the texts Paul wrote cannot be interpreted.

9.72. At the end of his modest monograph on Paul's relation to Judaism, Lüdemann (1983, p.42) asserts that 'Paul's apocalyptic and mythical picture of the world cannot be carried over by critical thinking into the present'. Lüdemann means not that Paul *cannot* be understood, but that Paul *needs* to be understood. If Paul is to be repeated, something else has also to be done, if it is to be shown that what has been repeated has been understood.

9.8. A theology consists of the combination of secular and religious terms.

9.81. By secular I mean, for example, 'table' (1 Cor.10:21); by religious, for example 'altar' (1 Cor.10:18). Or to take another example, 'sin' on the one hand and 'crime' on the other.

9.82. But we can give 'crime' a religious colouring if we translate it by 'transgression'. In Rom.5:14 the translators speak of 'the transgression of Adam'.

9.9. A theology consists of secular terms with the addition of qualifiers: there are tents and *holy* tents. Tak' tent! (sc. 'Note this distinction!' ⟨the language is the Scots'⟩).

9.91. In 2 Cor.5:1 Paul draws the distinction between a 'tent' and a 'house'.

9.92. But the 'house' is qualified: it is a 'house not made with hands'. It is one thing to live in a house not made with skilled hands. It is another thing to live in a house made with no hands at all.

9.93. When God is the subject of the sentence '... builds a house', he is not also the subject of the sentence 'with his hands ... lifts the bricks'.

9.94. Could God be the subject of the sentence 'With an outstretched arm (Dt.26:8) ... builds a house not made with hands'? For an arm after all is an arm even if there is no hand at the end of it.

9.95. In 2 Cor.5:1 Paul is drawing by implication a distinction between a 'house' and a 'house not made with hands'.

9.96. Explicitly he draws a distinction between a 'tent' and a 'house'. But the 'tent' is an *'earthly* tent'. So by implication he is drawing a distinction between that and a *'heavenly* tent'. Paul knew. He made them; the former, that is. The tents Paul made could have been called 'heavenly' not by stretch of the canvas, but by a stretch of the imagination.

9.97. The word 'heavenly' has already a religious colouring (not always maintained in the *Umgangssprache*, the 'everyday speech', of the English: 'That is a heavenly hat you are wearing'). The English language presents the translator with the alternative 'sky' or 'heaven'. One word in German applies indifferently to each: *'Himmel'*: 'sky' or 'heaven'.

9.98. Paul is contrasting a tent pitched on the ground (and subject to all the winds of change) with a house built in the sky, the sky being thought of as the place where God is located, where 'falls not hail, or rain, or any snow' (Tennyson, *The Passing of Arthur*).

9.99. Of course, if in the sky a house is built without hands, it is also likely that the sky in which the house is built is not made of atmosphere.

10.1. It is important to ask not only what Paul said and not only what he meant by saying it, but whether what he said is true.

10.11. Paul may of course not always have had the option of saying something different from what he did say. We may judge, for example, his views on homosexuality as invalid, but Paul's judgements precede a good deal of subsequent discussion, on biology, human and animal, on social anthropology and the like. Similarly, while he can say 'There is neither male nor female' (Gal.3:27), there are other of his statements that do not sound a clarion call to Lilith or to Mother Earth in the same way: 'The head of a woman is her husband' (1 Cor.11:3). But the social environment of Paul's thought and imagination may allow us only to say that what he said *was* true, or had at least *some* validity, but has it now no longer. Or maybe merely we should just reluctantly concede that he *nearly* did as well as he could have done.

10.12. But more importantly than the eternalization of Paul's prejudices or judgements on such matters as the emancipation of homosexuals and the liberation of women is the question of the mould within which his thought is cast. And here we might judge him not so much untrue as misleading: 'We who are alive ... shall be caught up ... to meet the Lord in the air' (1 Thess. 4:17).

10.13. But does Paul mislead? Or are we misled? For surely 'air' and 'clouds' and 'sky' should only be alerting us to the fact that Paul has his being in a symbolic universe; that he is using not 'picturing models' of the kind that occur in the maritime section of the municipal museum, but 'disclosure models' (Ramsey, 1964, p.10; and *passim*) that may be 'isomorphic' (Black, 1962, p.222) with what is modelled, but do not replicate it.

10.14. *Sachkritik*, 'material criticism', 'content criticism' (and a further string of barbarous appellations <Morgan, 1973, p.42>) has a better chance with the question of whether Paul was a universalist or not, the question whether God was capable of and was in fact going to be good to everyone and everything. For Paul seems to have been incapable of making up his mind on the question. God's concern for 'many' (Rom.5:19), we are told by Paul's commentators (e.g. Black, 1973, p.90), is God's concern for *all* ('By this accurate version some hurtful mistakes about partial redemption and absolute reprobation had been happily prevented' <Bentley, 1838, Vol.III, p.244, cit. Black, *ibid.*>). And yet Paul can also speak of 'vessels of wrath made for destruction' (Rom.9:22), on which O'Neill (1975, p.159), who reads perhaps too widely, can say that he, O'Neill, agrees with Calvin that this is Paul's thought but cannot agree with Calvin that the thought is 'admirable' (or agree with Paul that the thought is Paul's — O'Neill, again, has summoned his glossator).

10.2. A method, then (9.7.), is of no use unless it *does* something.

10.3. A theology, then (9.8.), consists of secular terms with the addition of qualifiers.

10.4. It is important, then (10.1.), to ask not only what Paul said and not only what he meant by saying it, but whether what he said is true.

10.5. But Paul has not said everything that ought to be said. For after all he is shorter than Proust or Plato.

10.51. Paul is silent on aesthetics and almost silent on sexuality (Mackinnon L. *obiter dictum*).

10.52. Where Paul *is* less then silent on sexuality (1 Cor.7) he should arguably have been as silent as a woman in church. If he had spoken at all, he should have said different things: 'the unmarried man is anxious about the affairs of the Lord ... the married man is anxious about worldly affairs ... (1 Cor.7:32 f)!

10.53. On the contrary. Without 'the society called a married couple', with 'the intention of jointly producing children' (Collingwood, 1942, p.165), there would soon be too few persons for the unmarried to convert: if no missionary position (*'Non consulare, inquies, dictum'*, 'You will say it (is) not the remark for a consular to make' <Cicero, *Letters to Atticus*, II.1>), no missionary expansion. One cannot change minds, if there are no minds to change.

10.54. It is said, of course, that Paul takes this view of marriage, because his view of the future is a limited one, because 'the ... time' is 'short' (1 Cor.7:29). If Paul thought so, he was wrong.

10.55. But *did* Paul think so? Was he speaking literally and wrongly — wrong about time and wrong about marriage? But religious people do not mean what they say; 'what is said is never, in religion as elsewhere, what is meant: the language never is the meaning' (Collingwood, 1924, p.130). Time is *symbolically* short? Paul means no more than that there are some decisions that brook no delay, that should not be deferred? And the decision not to get married is one of them? But what 'brooks no delay' must shortly be done. So the time *is* short.

10.56. Q.E.D.

10.57. But whether the time is long or short, the difference between being married and unmarried is not between being less religious and more religious, between 'caring for the things of the

Lord' and not so caring, but between being religious with wife and children and being religious without them.

10.58. And if it be conceded to Paul that it is difficult to be religious *with* them, it should also be symmetrically conceded that it is difficult to be religious *without* them. Paul's enthusiasm is 'a horrid thing ...' (5.84.).

10.6. In Philippians 2:5-11 '... who, though he was in the form of God, did not count equality with God a thing to be grasped ...', Paul sings a song.

10.61. He writes a song or writes down one he wrote earlier or that someone else wrote earlier.

10.62. It is a song sung to God or a song sung within the Christian movement. A song of this kind is called, according to the 'craftbound' (2.83.) conventions, a 'hymn'. If simultaneously a string is twanged, the string not of a military or toxic, but of a musical instrument, it is called a 'psalm'. Why should the devil have all the good instruments? Why the devil should all the good instruments be played elsewhere than in the meetings of the movement?

10.63. The Deutero-Pauline author or authors of Ephesians and Colossians add 'spiritual songs' to 'psalms' and 'hymns' (Eph.5:19, Col.3:16). A 'spiritual' song is a 'craftbound' song.

10.64. Each man versifies Paul's verses as he is able. There is no need here to add superabundance to what the scholars have abundantly produced. By a 'trade-agreement' there is a song, but no agreement on its verse-division. The surgeons disagree on where to 'ply the steel' (Eliot T.S.).

10.7. 'Hymnology', says Nock (1972, p.931), 'can precede theology and outrun it'. '... who, though he was in the form of God ...' etc., is not logically on all fours with 'Three times I have been shipwrecked ...' (2 Cor.11:25). 'On a clear day you can see forever', sings Streisand. 'The word became flesh', sings John or 'John'.

10.71. Paul may be singing a song about Adam or about Heracles. The rules of polysemy suggest that he may be doing both.

10.72. And, of course, he is singing about Jesus of Nazareth. He says as much; 'who' (v.6) has an antecedent and Jesus is named in v.10.

10.73. Named and acclaimed: 'Mr. Jesus' or 'Master Jesus'.

10.74. The title 'Mr.' or 'Master' is very fluid and can belong with equal ease to the linguistic realms of courtesy, slavery and divinity, to specify just three. The last, in my submission, is not in question: 'When all things are subjected to him (sc. Jesus), then the Son himself (sc. Jesus) will also be subjected to him (sc. God) who put all things under him (sc. Jesus) (1 Cor.15:28).

10.8. If in the *Carmen Christi*, the song about Jesus in Phil.2:6-11, Jesus is being compared and contrasted with Adam; if the passage denotes Jesus and connotes Adam, then we need to know something about Adam, if we are going to understand more fully the song Paul is singing; or perhaps the song Paul is recording.

10.81. Adam is the leading character in a piece of narrative fiction (Gen.1-3) with which Paul was familiar. The story, in the way stories do, makes a number of points. Of these I select two: (1) all men are mortal; (2) all men are bad.

10.82. Adam belongs to the realm of fiction and Jesus to the realm of fact. Fiction is being compared and contrasted with fact.

10.83. But fiction about Adam refers, in the way that fiction refers, to facts of human experience, viz. (1) that all men are mortal..., etc. In this sense, fact is being compared with fact.

10.84. The story about Adam has imaginative form. The story is an expression of the literary imagination.

10.85. What is said about Jesus is also the expression of imagination; not the expression of the historical imagination, but of the literary imagination. A song is a poem with musical accompaniment.

10.86. Paul's historical imagination, it is true, is given *some* exercise. He includes history, alludes to it, touches on it, for Jesus 'humbled himself and became obedient unto death, even death on a cross' (v.8). Jesus' life was not an exhibition of over-ruling power' (Whitehead, 1927, p.47) and ended in his execution. But the word 'obedient' takes us outside historical study and into theology. Paul's poem is a religious poem. It is a poem that depicts God as agent: 'Therefore God has highly exalted him'. The imagination is literary; it is also theological. Or, what amounts to the same thing, the poem is theological literature.

10.87. And the story about Adam is literary and theological: Gen.1-3 is a story and a story about God.

10.88. In Phil.2 a story is in juxtaposition to a poem: Gen.1-3 to Phil.2, a story about Adam to a poem about Jesus. In this sense we are dealing with two fictions.

10.89. This is not to deny that we are dealing with facts, but only to assert that we are dealing with them by the mode of fiction, which is perhaps the only mode for dealing with such facts as these.

10.9. Heracles, too, may be among the connotations of what Paul says here. Jesus is denoted; Adam, maybe, connoted; maybe also Heracles.

10.91. Paul does not tell us that Jesus' father was replaced by God. Nor does he tell us that Heracles' father was replaced by Zeus.

10.92. Neither does he tell us that Jesus was or was held to be a 'drunkard' (Mt.11:19). Nor that Heracles took to or is said to have taken to his cups: 'and at a banquet, when his (sc. Eurytus') guest (sc. Heracles) was full of wine, he (Eurytus) thrust him (Heracles) from his doors' (Sophocles, *Trachiniae* 268).

10.93. Paul does offer a punctiliar summation of Jesus' career, he tells in two words Jesus' life-story: Jesus 'emptied himself' (Phil.2:7). And this is as much as to say that Jesus paradigmatically instantiates benevolence (6.34.). Or, if 'our conception of autonomous agents is of beings who can say 'I shall do', 'I do', or 'I have done', and this 'I' injects a permanent note of egocentricity into the whole system' (Lucas, 1976, p.44), then Jesus instantiates not egocentricity, but its negation.

10.94. Pindar (*Nemeans* 1:62 ff) tells us what Teiresias said Heracles would do, 'how many lawless monsters he would slay on the dry land and how many upon the sea ... that there was one most hateful, one who walked in the crooked path of envy, whom he would do to death (sc. Antaeus) ... that when the gods shall meet the giants in battle on the plain of Phlegra, their foes shall soon find their bright tresses befouled with dust beneath that hero's rushing arrows, but he himself, at rest from mighty labours, shall have allotted to him, as his choicest prize, peace that would endure for ever in the homes of bliss, where on receiving Hebe as his blushing bride, and celebrating the marriage feast, he shall glorify his hallowed home in the presence of Zeus, the son of Cronus'. 'The old-Dorian hero, slayer of monsters, purger of the earth, who triumphs over the terrors of Hades, and brings the apples of immortality from the garden of the Hesperides' (Jebb, 1892, p.x) provides a parallel to the career of Jesus. Without pursuing further here the language of Pindar and his interpreters (Deas, 1931), we may agree that, in presenting us with Heracles and Jesus, literature or Paul and Pindar and their like present us with a pair of problem solvers: both, for instance, so to speak, 'brought apples'; or brought fullness where emptiness was before.

10.95. *If* Paul is moving or is also moving in this *milieu*, he is claiming that the aspirations expressed in the Heraclean/Herculean literature are satisfied by Jesus.

11.1. The name 'Heracles' is theophoric: 'Heracles' means 'the glory of Hera'.

11.11. The name 'Christ', if 'Christ' *is* by Paul's time a name and not a title, is also theophoric: Jesus is 'the one anointed by God', 'the anointee of God'.

11.12. Heracles has a fluid status (as well as a fluid intake <10.92.>). By virtue of his theophoric name, he ought to be a hero, a man whose life is larger than the common lot, but 'by a bold combination of terms' (Farnell, 1921, p.95), Pindar (*Nemeans* 3:22) calls him 'that hero and god'. 'We know, adds Farnell (*ibid.*), 'that the term *theos* was often vaguely and thoughtlessly applied by the *littérateurs* of Greece, but the claim of Heracles' divinity is not in doubt, for 'the usual Attic sacrifice to Heracles appears to have been of the 'Olympian' type, the ox being lifted from the ground and his neck drawn back' (Farnell, 1921, p.97) and in Tarsus Heracles was identified with the god (God?) Sandan or Sandas. Josephus, moreover, tells us (*Ant.* 8.5.3, par.146, cit. Farnell, p.168) that in Tyre Heracles' 'awakening' (*egersis*) was celebrated in January and a series of coins suggest the like for Tarsus. But this last point, though interesting, is not decisive, for a god can go to sleep and waken as a god, a man can go to sleep and waken as a man.

11.13. And a reader go to sleep as something less than a man and waken in the usual way.

11.2. Is the status of Jesus similarly ambiguous?

11.21. In particular, do the words 'in the form of God' (Phil.2:6) assert or, though occurring in a song, nevertheless allow us to assert that Jesus was a god or God?

11.22. The monotheism of 'God the father' suggests that Jesus was neither, unless in this case one God can consist of two persons.

11.23. The question, of course, is what we can make of Paul's mind here and not of the mind of someone who is attempting to define or to recognize the worth of Heracles, to decide whether his worth is more than the worth of His Worship (by etymology: 'Worth-ship') the Mayor and, if so, how much '*mair*' (sc. 'more' <Scots>) — Jesus as a King of kings and Mayor of mayors.

11.24. The word 'form' slips and slides into 'shape', 'appearance', 'what something looks like'. A text from Josephus (*Ap.*2.190, cit. *TWNT* 4, pp.749f, highlighted by Grelot <1972, p.505>) suggests we might add such words as 'magnitude', 'manifestation', 'image' and 'similarity'. To a visitor the court of Solomon would have appeared in all its 'glory', for 'glory' too is cognate with these others.

11.25. Dresses are shapeless or have shape. The Hermes of Praxiteles has form. What form does God take, the God of 'Abraham, Isaac and Jacob', the God of the Jews and the Christians?

11.26. Hebrew iconoclasm does not always appear in the verbal field. Their attitude to images does not preclude recourse to imagery. Where Hermes is an athlete, the 'father' and 'judge' of Paul suggest a custodial mien and protective clasp. Such is God's shape.

11.27. Everything that is appears to be something, or appears as something, though some things may not be what they appear to be. An appearance can be a *mere* appearance.

11.28. But not here: what he appears to be, God is. It is *this* that Paul appears to be saying.

11.29. But what is in question, is not whether God's form is in conformity with what God is, nor, at least primarily, whether the form of Jesus is comparable with the form of Heracles either before or after his apokolokyntosis, but whether the form Jesus had or has is the form that God had or has. Murphy-O'Connor suggests (1976), though he is looking at the song before it reached Paul's lips (but what reason is there for thinking that the song's meaning changed when it reached them?): being 'in the form of God' means that men ought to look like God and that Jesus did look like him, 'for Jesus is the authentic embodiment of humanity' (*op. cit.*, p.41). And this makes Jesus God no more than it made Adam God or than it made or makes God or gods any other or some or all of either the sons of men or the daughters of women.

11.3. 'Ecclesiology' means thinking about the church. And 'church' is the name, the 'craftbound' name, of the Christian movement, for other reasons and in so far as it is organized.

11.31. The word 'organization', at this early period, is probably to be taken with a pinch of salt or, what amounts to very much the same thing, *cum grano salis*. But the movement had already administrators (1 Cor.12:28), its leaders, its 'cybernetics' (Greek: *kuberneseis*). *'Eppur'*', one might have observed, '*si muove*', 'and yet it moves'; Eliot's Hippopotamus, not resting on his belly in the mud, was already taking 'feeble steps ... Ascending (indeed) from the damp savannas ...'.

11.4. The whole organization was to behave as an organism; the whole corporation as a 'body' (1 Cor.12:27). Paul's pictorial imagination is not slow to appropriate this 'ancient commonplace' (Black, 1973, p.153). The working of one body is analogous to the working of a number of bodies. Different people can co-operate, much as a brain can instruct a foot to move to a place where a hand can manipulate.

11.41. The genitive 'of Christ' in the phrase 'the body of Christ' tells us very little about the way Paul thought that Jesus of Nazareth was related to the Christian movement. Works on prepositions are reliable only as interruptions to our labours. Let Deissmann (1892) mark this, for he 'has virtually declared that religion resides in the prepositions' (so Stewart, 1935, pp.154 f, cit. Moule, 1963, p.48).

11.42. On how Jesus is related to the Christian movement Paul has more than one thing to say.

11.43. The movement may be conceived as a fraternity, a band of brothers, of whom Jesus is the eldest ('... that he might be the first-born of many brethren' Rom.8:29).

11.44. If Paul's word *doulos*, which, to speak in abstraction from any context, can be indifferently translated as either 'slave' or 'servant', can sometimes or often or ever be taken to mean the former, then the relation between Jesus and Paul and, by extension from Paul, the movement as a whole is conceived as the relation between a slave and a slave-master. We might *then* turn in triumph to the grammar-book for a 'genitive of possession': 'the body of Christ' is the body the master possesses, is Jesus' 'talking tool' (*instrumenti genus vocale* <Varro, cit. de Vaux, 1961, p.80>), Jesus' property with locomotive abilities.

11.5. 'Spirit' *(esprit)* is a model of divine activity: God is active in so far as he *breathes*, as in the story (Gen.2:7) he breathed into the nostrils of Adam, or *blows* either a gale as upon Captain MacWhirr and Jukes in Conrad's *Typhoon*, such that 'in and around the gale' (for gales have their circumferences?) 'occurred a cosmic disclosure' (Ramsey, 1973, pp.3 f) or a breeze, 'how unfailing a friend ... the forenoon wind from the sea ... strongest just after noon', who does not leave you till the need for his freshness passes away with the sunset' (Adam Smith, 1894, p.67, cit. Ramsey, *ibid.*, pp.5 f).

11.51. But it may be objected that what a word once meant may not be what it now means. There is, that is, the *genetic* fallacy. But, though 'spirit' as 'air in motion' is at least some way below the surface of Paul's thought, it might be rash to deny its presence altogether. Is it altogether irrelevant to note how close it is to the surface of John's: 'And when he (sc. Jesus) had said this, he *breathed* on them, and said to them 'Receive the Holy Spirit'' (20:22).

11.52. When a man has wind inside him, he may be said (to be in need of medical help or) to be animated. And there are some modes of behaviour that may be described as 'suranimated', as we may surmise for the boy wrestler, who was forced to sue his opponent after the final for the sum (3.000 *drachmae*) which his opponent had promised him before it in return for his agreement to lose it (Harris, 1964, p.47), or as we may surmise rather for the poet, for the hero and for the administrator. But 'suranimated' is rather, of course, Teilhard de Chardin's word (1960, p.100 <Dr. O'Donoghue kindly located this reference>).

11.53. Or perhaps one may speak very generally of a *savoir faire* and a *pouvoir faire*, of knowing how to act and being able to do so; of intelligence and capacity; and then their realization in action.

11.54. When a god or God has wind inside him, he can expel it and by that expulsion impel others, much as a 'kiss of life' can bring about the recovery of a nearly drowned man.

11.55. Or when God has wind inside him, he can be said to be animated or suranimated and can cause, by analogy with the historical sense of the word 'cause' (Collingwood, 1940, pp.290 ff) animation or suranimation in others. He can tell others what to do and enable them to do it.

11.6. Nouns in theology can often usefully be construed as verbs. 'Spirit' is one of these. A single noun, it is as multiply pregnant as the Empress of Blandings (8.9.). It licenses an extended family of propositions, such as: 'God breathes', '... animates', '... enables', etc. God, able himself, is able to enable.

11.61. The noun 'spirit' is prolific of a family of propositions as plastic containers on the sand of the seashore for multitude.

11.62. Thus we may say in summary of the propositions thus spawned that 'God acts', with the proviso that what is being summarised could hardly be enumerated.

11.63. And God's activity may be characterized, provided that we show no great confidence in knowing what is being characterized and how the terms we use to characterize it apply to it.

11.64. We may say if we like that God's activity is intelligent and effective. And we may add what we are enabled to infer from Paul's love song in 1 Cor.13 that it is agapeistic. But there is no guarantee that our criteria for intelligence, effectiveness and love will allow us to detect that activity when it occurs, for we do not 'know', as Paul points out (1 Cor.13:12), but we 'know' only 'in part'.

11.7. The word 'activity' when applied to God is itself a model. The model is historical, drawn from our study of human action.

11.71. When we examine the thought and action of members of the Christian movement, the body ecclesiastic, as Paul asks us to examine it in 1 Cor.12, we are directed to a variety of activities that range from ecstasy to administration, even if these are only activities in so far as the agents are allowing themselves to be *acted on*; are patients.

11.72. Whatever those activities are that Paul there cites, he construes them as 'caused' (11.55.) by God's activity.

11.8. If Paul tells us that there are those in Corinth who 'speak with tongues', we might reply that it is hardly possible to speak with anything else.

11.81. Should Paul then impatiently rejoin that he is making use of an abbreviation, that ought to be well known, for 'speaking with the tongues of angels', we might have to pause before maintaining that entities multiplied beyond necessity can hardly permit a laryngological analysis, to say nothing of the rhino-otological difficulties that may also be involved.

11.82. We might have to pause simply to recognise that Paul at time T1 presupposed what some of us now at time T2 have learnt to stop presupposing. Paul *illinc et tunc*, 'there and then', presupposed that 'angels' were, in Whitehead's phrase, 'actual entities'.

11.83. But it is arguable that Paul presupposed nothing of the sort, that Paul was as aware as we are of the gap between sense and reference in the language-game in which 'God' is the presiding category. If Paul knows that he does not know, he knows in part the limits of the language he is using.

11.84 But if he knows in part, it is also arguable that he does not wholly know that religion is 'thought growing up in the husk of language, and as yet unconscious that language and thought are different things' (Collingwood, 1924, p.125).

11.85. But however one judges Paul judged the logical status of his epistolary propositions, if to say even so much is not to introduce undue sophistication into a context where naïvety may rather have been the order of the day, Paul would certainly have agreed that between the sky and the ground there occurs communication, that there are messages that come down from the sky, that there are messages that pass from God's mouth to men's ears, even if it should remain unsettled between Paul and ourselves whether or not these messages are carried by messengers.

11.86. Anyone who has any acquaintance with infants knows that they are capable of significant pre-linguistic noise. There is no reason why there should not be contexts where adults, who in other contexts are capable of linguistic expression, feel content to emit expressive sound, the *Aha-Erlebnis* or 'Aha-experience', for example.

11.87. 'Nevertheless', Paul tells us (1 Cor.14:19), 'in church I would rather speak five words with my mind ... than ten thousand words in a tongue'. He probably spoke more.

11.88. Of these morphemes , or phonemes rather, for we are dealing not with formed words, but with a series of distinguishable sounds, God is reckoned to be the cause.

11.89. Omitting the 'tongues of angels' as imaginary, as mere imagery, we may speak imaginatively of God's tongue, communicating with men, who in their turn use their tongues to speak to God or to men on God's behalf. 'Hear the words of God or hear at least his phonemes'. The term 'tongue' is more concrete, less abstract than 'communication'. Sometimes there are words, to speak *deo remoto*, 'with God removed', to speak *etsi deus non daretur*, 'as if God were not given', and sometimes mere sounds, that spring unbidden to the mind or to the heart, of whose reasons the reason knows nothing, like the *alienatio mentis*, 'estrangement from one's own mind', of the Dionysiac cult (Rohde, 1925, p.259). There are occasions when one's mind goes abroad.

11.9. Paul's religious language is secular language within religious brackets.

11.91. Whether or not the world within which Paul imagines and thinks is accurately described as a world of 'primitive pansacrality' (Von Rad, 1975, vol.1, p.374) the interpreter is not spared the analysis of what is so described.

12.1. Jesus of Nazareth is not now alive in the sense that historians can say he was alive in the period that succeeds his birth and precedes his death, the post-natal, pre-mortem period.

12.11. The sense in which Jesus was alive at that period and the sense in which the historian of Jesus is now alive provide the empirical bases for the word 'alive', for speaking of Jesus' non-empirical or post-mortem 'life'. The word 'life' for the dead is borrowed from or 'displaced' from (Schon, 1963) the life of the living.

12.2. The English language includes the words 'mind' and 'body'. One is speaking more obviously of the second when one speaks of a man's hand or his foot than when one speaks of someone's intelligence or his power , though it is hard to see that one could speak of the latter in the absence of the former.

12.3. In Rom.8:9 ff Paul speaks of having 'the Spirit of Christ'. In the same context he speaks, with apparent indifference, of 'God' and 'the Spirit of God'.

12.31. Concerning Jesus of Nazareth he means two things: that Jesus is not now bodily alive in the way that he once was; and that the kind of intelligence and effectiveness that is transmitted to his companions in the Christian movement or by the 'contagion' with which, to use Van Buren's metaphor (1963, pp.152 f), his companions are infected is the kind of intelligence that is found in God's 'head' and the kind of power that is effected by God's 'arm'.

12.32. But Paul uses here (Rom.8:9 ff) of course neither the vocabulary of 'transmission' nor of 'contagion', but of 'being in', 'having' and 'being indwelt by' or 'being inhabited by'.

12.33. 'Dwelling', to speak only of the last, licenses us by etymology to speak of Paul's 'ecology' (oikein is 'to dwell' or 'have a habitat'). A rather prosaic analysis suggests that the relation between the Christian and Jesus of Nazareth is analogous to the relation between a house and its occupant. Less prosaic parallels can be found in Plato (The Palatine Anthology V,78):

> 'My soul was on my lips as I was kissing Agathon.
> Poor soul! she came hoping to cross over to him.'

and in Donne:

> 'Our eye-beames twisted, and did thred
> Our eyes, upon one double string ...' (The Exstasie).

In her annotations on this 'interinanimation', 'this dialogue of one', Gardiner (1965, p.262) cites Ficino (1944, pp.221 f) in Burton's version (The Anatomy of Melancholy, part 3, sect. 2, memb. 2, subs. 2):

> 'Lycias he stares on Phaedrus face, and Phaedrus fastens the balls of his eys upon Lycias, and with those sparkling rays sends out his spirits. The beams of Phaedrus eys are easily mingled with the beams of Lycias, and spirits are joined to spirits. This vapour begot in Phaedrus heart, enters into Lycias bowels: and that which is a greater wonder, Phaedrus blood is in Lycias heart'.

and cites (ibid., p.185) Leone Ebreo (1937, p.260):

> 'Each one being transformed into the other becomes two, at once lover and beloved; and two multiplied by two makes four, so that each of them is twain, and both together are one and four'.

12.4. 'Abraham believed God', Paul tells us (Rom.4:3), 'and it was reckoned to him as righteousness'.

12.41. Paul was not the first to tell us this, but the author or authors of Genesis 15:6.

12.5. 'History', Collingwood tells us (1940, p.56), 'has its own rubric', namely 'the evidence at our disposal obliges us to conclude that such and such an event happened'.

12.51. 'There is also', Collingwood goes on, 'a rubric for use in narrating legends ...: 'the story says that ...', or 'now the story goes on to say that ...'. Where the reader is assumed to know the ropes these rubrics are left out'.

12.52. The Abraham story is a legend and the rubric has been left out.

12.6. This story is, in Thucydides' phrase (I.22), 'a possession for ever'. It has been found to be worth re-telling and re-reading.

12.61. The literary historian attempts to re-construct the context in which a story was first told.

12.62. For the first context of Gen.15:6 of particular importance, Von Rad suggests (1958, pp.130 ff), are the declarations about or reckonings of animals and men as 'clean' or 'unclean', as unfit, or fit, or the like, which were pronounced by cultic functionaries or priests. It was the task of these functionaries to look a gift-horse in the mouth.

12.63. The declaration or assessment in Gen.15:6 is made not by officials but by God. And positive vetting is given not to a man as free from illness, nor to an animal as free from defects, but to a man who has 'faith'.

12.65. Positive vetting is accorded to a man in a story who accords a positive vetting to God. The man is convinced that he will have children, and that these children will have children. This conviction occurs to him.

12.66. To move from the individual to the tribe, the nation is convinced it has a future. That, I take it, is what the story refers to. For just as Adam is both the name of an individual man and Man or womankind, so Abraham is also or can (wrongly) be taken to be 'father of a crowd' (rightly: 'exalted father'). The significant pun is as familiar to the Pentateuch as to Derrida. Punning belongs to the generative grammar of Hebrew theology.

12.67. Paul is not the sort of man who discusses his central terms (he is almost the sort of man who does not discuss anything). But I take it that by 'faith' he means 'trust'; that he is using a term that belongs to the field of personal relations: trust is appropriately reposed in one who is trustworthy.

12.7. But someone will say, 'You have said that before'.

12.71 But can it be said too often?

12.8. In talking of 'faith' Paul is not being theriomorphic: he is not asserting that God has feathers; nor physeomorphic: he is not asserting that God has crystalline structure, has the solidity of sedimentary strata, though that currency would have value. He is being anthropomorphic.

12.9. Paul contrasts 'faith' with 'works'.

12.91. God has 'worked' Paul's acquittal; Paul has not 'worked' innocently. The judge acquits Paul not because Paul has acted innocently, but because the judge has acted myopically. The judge has turned the telescope to his blind eye.

12.92. In Gen.15:6 Abraham notes what God can do and that what God can, he will. *Verbum meum pactum*: God's 'word', as in the City (sc. of London), is his 'bond'.

12.93. Abraham is convinced that the circumstances will arise in which his sexual potency will move to sexual act, that his sexual activity will lead to sexual fertility.

13.1. Trust can be contrasted with its absence. Abraham would not have got a positive verdict, had he not trusted, had he dithered.

13.11. But that is to make God's verdict conditional on Abraham's recognition of God's reliability. It is to say that the verdict was caused by the recognition. It is to read a sentence that consists of two clauses co-ordinated by 'and': 'Abraham believed and ...' as a sentence that consists of a main clause and a subordinate clause introduced by 'because': 'it was reckoned to him as righteousness, because Abraham believed'.

13.12. God forbid! Protestantism forbids!

13.13. What the story should have said is that God evaluated Abraham positively and Abraham's confidence in the future flowed from this. The verdict, in the *patois* of theology (2.93.), is 'prevenient' and Abraham's reaction is subsequent. 'Only those who are loved can love' (Bultmann, 1953, p.32). Abraham is acquitted at the bar of God's justice, not because Abraham recognised that justice for what it was, but because that judge is an acquitting judge.

13.2. There were resources available for Abraham that enabled him to face the future. 'God' is the term used by those whose task it is to give an account of such matters, whose task it is to indicate from where these resources derive. Abraham is enabled by that which enables him. And the future would be bleak enough without it.

13.21. It is bleak enough with it. 'In hope', Paul tells us (Rom.4:18),

Abraham believed 'against hope'.

3.3.   'Faith' regarded as a secular term relates a man to other men or to a context in which he finds himself. If it has been so regarded, when it occurs as an element of religious discourse, it has been transferred or 'metaphored' from the one realm to the other. 'Faith' is a metaphor from human relations.

3.31.   The correlative of 'one who trusts' is 'one who is trustworthy' (3.32.).

3.32.   God can be 'the one who is trustworthy'. Can he be 'the one who trusts'? Does God have 'faith'?

3.33.   While God should find the future bleak, there are analytical reasons for supposing that he does not find it altogether bleak. For if the future is that than which nothing bleaker can be thought, then God is that to which the future is not altogether bleak. Bleakness is not all, but ripeness. In that sense, God has 'faith'.

3.34.   But there are grounds for supposing that God does not trust men as far as he can throw them, if Paul's dictum is true, that 'all have sinned' (Rom.3:23), or its forensic analogue, that 'all men are criminals'.

13.35.   And yet, even if Paul does not say so (and a little sheaf of letters from 'the pocket-book that contains the sacred writings of Christianity' <Vermes, 1981, p.1> does not leave him time to say very much about anything), God could be said to be related to men, if 'against faith', also 'in faith'; in trust and against it; or against it, but also in it: God trusts men against his better judgement.

13.4.   The Pauline correlate of trust is 'grace'.

13.41.   Milton somewhere, lost somewhere in *Paradise Lost*, speaks of Satan as being bound on a '*bad* errand'. God is bound on good ones.

13.42.   Drilling under the banner of 'grace', we may suppose that God is well disposed and performs well. The metaphor again is inter-personal.

13.43.   The mystery here, as elsewhere, is not the word 'grace', but God. 'Grace' focusses the blur.

13.44.   'Grace' in the secular sphere is a well-known, if not so well-instantiated, phenomenon. Kings, slave-masters and gentlemen have all been known to be or conceived of as owing to be 'gracious'. The word, of course, has a slightly archaic ring, but that should only serve to endear it to *homo religiosus*.

13.5.   'Grace' concentrates meaning , much as a black hole concentrates matter. The phenomenon of 'condensation' (Turner,

1970, pp.28 ff; Turner and Turner, 1978, p.246) is here at its height. The word, like many Pauline words, becomes a synonym for, an 'abbreviation' (5.9.) for Christianity.

13.51. If this is true, a commentary on 'grace' will be as brief as an explanation of Christianity.

13.52. Or does the word 'grace' attack Christianity from a particular direction?

13.6. Paul thinks of his career less as a course of action that he has chosen than as a privilege conferred; and conferred on him not by the caliphs (can there be more than one of these?) of Jerusalem, such 'pillars' (Gal.2:9) of the community as James, Peter and John. The characteristic 'voice' of the Christian verb is the passive: not 'I have chosen', but 'I am chosen'. (And, despite Paul, the characteristic 'number' is the first person plural: 'we are chosen'.)

13.61. Were we to speak of 'grace' forensically, we might say that the 'judge' exercises the prerogative of mercy.

13.62. But should we speak so? For 'father' and such cognate images that bear a family-resemblance to the familial ones keep up constant pressure on forensic terms and are always driving them from the field.

13.63. The implicate of 'grace' is freedom. We are not paid domestics; we belong to, are members of the family — and mature members at that.

13.64. Jesus was a free, or more or less a free man (for was he free entirely from the defects of a symmetrical dualism <4.5.>: 'if there are those who are in, then there are those who are out'?).

13.65. We may infer from the way Jesus was treated that other free men are liable to be treated in the same way. *Ab esse ad posse consequentia valet,* from the fact that he was may be derived the possibility that we may. The inference is further confirmed by casting a cool eye on other segments of human history.

13.66. Being a free member of God's family may result in conflict both with those who are 'not family' or who do not yet think of themselves as such and with those who are.

13.67. But Paul's terminal symbolism comprises peace, not war and life, not death: a symbolic nexus arrived at by the operation of the imagination at its ideal limits.

13.68. 'Grace' is that which enables the militia to survive defeat, which enabled Paul, despite the catalogue of imprisonments and loss of sleep (2 Cor.11:23 ff), to trek from near Damascus to Rome, like Peter Pienaar, in John Buchan's *Mr. Standfast,* 'who trekked solitary from the Garungoze to the Limpopo with fever and a broken arm ..' (*cit.* Dodd, 1920, in the title pages).

13.7. Theology demands the use of three tenses: past, present and future (1.32.).

13.71. While the discussion of any particular theological point may not need the use of more than one tense, the discussion of 'grace', of God's benevolence and beneficence, requires two: God helps Paul; he also helped Jesus.

13.72. The assertion that benevolence and beneficence characterises God's activity supports the analogical argument: 'As God helps me, so he helped Jesus'. God is a steady sort of character.

13.73. Paul usually, I think, reverses the analogy: 'As God helped Jesus, so he helps me'. If God's actions are usually in character, it would not much matter which way Paul argued.

13.8. Does God *do anything?*

13.81. When speaking of the activity of God, it is important to keep a firm grasp on the empirical-historical facts of the matter; to stand on the firm ground of history and firmly grasp its soil. Someone in *Gone With The Wind* does this.

13.82. During a thunderstorm a character in *The Lady's Not For Burning* (Fry, 1950, p.33) speaks of 'the morose dynamics of our dumb friend, Jehovah'. God rumbles; he does not speak. Does he then act?

13.83. Of the empirical-historical facts of the matter in relation to which Paul introduces the word 'grace', to prescind from more, I here select two: 'I am not getting enough sleep' (2 Cor.11:27 *agrupniais* 'through many sleepless night') and 'Jesus of Nazareth was executed by some combination of Jews and Romans' (Rom.3:24 'They are justified by his grace as a gift through the redemption which is in Christ Jesus, whom God put forward as an expiation through his blood').

13.84. As examples of the instantiation of 'grace', loss of sleep, relatively trivial, and execution, seemingly terminal, are both uncomfortable. It should be possible to choose more comforting examples. Perhaps Paul saw a sunset in Ephesus, as he 'tired' him 'with talking and sent him down the sky' (7.1.). Paul does not tell us this, but I expect that Renan's Paul does. Or did he ever take wine for the sake of the vintage and not just for the sake of the stomach? Ποῖος ξέρει; 'Who knows?' I expect Renan does, for a man that can tell us that Jesus 'constantly rode about ... upon a mule, 'that favourite riding-animal of the East, which is so docile and sure-footed and whose great dark eyes, shaded by long lashes, are full of gentleness'' (Schweitzer, 1911, p.184 <citing Renan>) is almost bound to be able to tell us anything.

13.85. Nevertheless, even in uncomfortable circumstances, Paul and Jesus kept going.

13.86. All the way to the Limpopo (13.68.) and across it to the other side.

13.87. It would be unsurprising if Paul had his 'off' days as well as his 'on' days. His remark about the Jews, that 'God's wrath has come upon them at last' (1 Thess.2:16), if it is not put down to a function of his 'symmetrical dualism' (13.64.), could be put down to one of his 'off' days: 'he got out of bed the wrong side' (Nineham, *obiter dictum*). But we may nevertheless agree that despite lack of sleep and his other natural and unnatural shocks Paul seems to have been able to keep going. And so did Jesus, despite his 'off' days too (?), despite the 'shadow of death' and despite, too, Paul tells us (here moving beyond the brief of the empirical-historical) its substance: 'Heads of the characters', Paul tells us, 'hammer through daisies' (Dylan Thomas, *And Death Shall Have No Dominion*).

13.88. Paul may not always have been very charming, but he did play *Follow My Leader* and he kept going.

13.9. Cognate with 'grace' is 'gift'.

13.91. As men give presents to God, a goat, say, or a stook, so God gives presents to men, the rest of the flock, say, or the stooks.

13.92. Paul regards Jesus as a *datum*, as a gift that has been given; and given, for the passive tense is 'divine', by God.

13.93. It is more natural to speak of a man as a giver of gifts than to speak of a man as himself a gift. Jesus, one might say, brought to the human race the inestimable gifts of freedom and brotherhood. One might even say that he gave himself to the task of liberation and the promotion of the brotherhood of man.

13.94. What Paul is suggesting is that the situation in which a giver A gives a gift B to a recipient C can be used as a model that relates God (A) to the human race (C) by Jesus (B). To speak in this way is odd, but not unintelligible. 'Jesus is God's gift to men' is an abbreviation for something like the following: Jesus offered the human race freedom and brotherhood; God offered (and offers) the human race freedom and brotherhood; God 'sired' (so to speak) Jesus of Nazareth and caused him to offer the human race freedom and brotherhood. So God gave the one who gave freedom and brotherhood.

14.1. An important parenthesis may perhaps be appended: the birth, life and death of Jesus of Nazareth are historical data; in terms of the model of the giving of presents they are theological data: on the assumption not only that Jesus, between his birth and his death, was alive, but is 'alive' in a sense that is metaphorically or analogically related to the first, God is to be imagined not only as *qui dedit*, 'the giver who gave a gift', but as a *dans*, 'the giver who is giving'; and Jesus not only as a *datum* or *datus*, 'a gift that has been given' or 'someone given as a gift', but as *qui datur*, 'one who is being given' — the Montanist point again (6.14.). This is an alternative way of saying or is an attempt to explicate, or 'unpack', to use the portmanteau metaphor, what I take Bultmann to be after by such a phrase as 'the paradoxical identity of a historical and an eschatological event'. 'Eschatology' covers a multitude of sins. These are some of the sins that Bultmann covers. 'The heavenly silt accumulates' (Gregor Smith *obiter scriptum*). And needs stirring.

14.2. There is nothing odd in speaking of two friends as 'at one'. And there should be nothing odd in speaking of two enemies as 'at two', though what we usually say is that they are 'at odds'.

14.21. With God we may be at odds or at one; in actual fact, probably *more or less* at odds or at one. The alternatives should not be too clear. There are some topics (and some disciplines?) where clarity and distinctness are not warranted. And some writers, one might add, for whom they are not possible.

14.22. However difficult to achieve in practice, and however rarely achieved, the idea that two men who are at odds should learn to walk together or become reconciled presents to comprehension no insuperable problems.

14.23. Complexities arise when into this plain context there is introduced the metaphor of animal sacrifice (5.1. ff).

14.3. Paul says that Jesus 'died for all' (2 Cor.5.14 f).

14.31. To the extent that the phrase 'died for all' is an ellipse for 'died as an animal sacrifice for', we may now ignore it, except in so far as that only is true which is said more than twice: 'What I say three times is true' (Lewis Carroll, *The Hunting of the Snark*).

14.32. 'Died for all' is also an ellipse for 'Jesus attempted to live for all and died in the attempt'.

14.33. Paul's talk of the death of Jesus is a synecdoche for the beginning and middle of what his death ended. It is usually, it should be added, said in the context of the beginning, middle and end of what *began* at his death.

14.34. Paul's speaking of 'all' refers in the first instance to those of his contemporaries who knew him, then to those of his successors who were coming to or could come to know him, in (either or both) his pre- and post-mortem modes, and then, on the assumption that while death may *appear* to be the end of life it is not the end either of Jesus' 'life' or of other men's 'lives' (sc. 'life' and 'lives' in the analogical sense), to those who precede him. The law of perishing, Paul might have said, is only *prima facie*. Jesus' historical predecessors become metaphorically his contemporaries; so he died for them, too, in the sense meant here, namely, he was killed in his attempt to benefit them.

14.35. In a footnote to the *Investigations*, Wittgenstein tells us (1958, p.11): 'Imagine a picture representing a boxer in a particular stance. Now this picture can be used to tell someone how he should stand, should hold himself; or how he should not hold himself; or how a particular man did stand in such-and-such a place; and so on ...'. *Via* the modes of song, story, anecdote and the like (and how clearly and distinctly do such modes *refer?*) it is possible to tell how Jesus lived. But that is not only how that man lived; it is how men ought to live. How Jesus stood is how I ought to stand.

14.36. But of the two sentences : 'He lived in such a way' and 'Live in such a way!', or of Braun's simpler analogues (8.4.) 'You may' (sc. because Jesus lived and 'lives' in such a way) and 'You ought' (sc. to live as Jesus lived or 'lives'), the former or indicative takes primacy over the latter or imperative. It does not much matter how I live. Or it does not matter so much. How Jesus stood is how I ought to stand, but, more importantly than how I ought to stand, is how *he* stood and stands.

14.37. Jesus boxed and boxes, not as my opponent, but as my sparring partner. If I box badly, he will not drub me or knock me out.

14.38. The athletic metaphor here models, first, pre-mortem facts and, second, post-mortem facts: there are facts and 'facts'.

14.4. 'Death' is an apt metaphor to describe the kind of life that led to Jesus' death. The same point might be made literally by saying that Jesus 'did not please himself' (Rom.15:3).

14.41. The transition from desire to choice, Collingwood tells us (1942, pp.91 ff), is made, negatively, by an 'act of refusing to let oneself be dictated to by desire' and, positively, by 'the acceptance of unhappiness'. 'Since', Collingwood goes on , 'the desiring self simply consists of the practical 'urge' from unhappiness to happiness, this act is a cutting off all that is going on in the life of the man who does it; as a kind of suicide, it goes by a name intolerably debased in the passage from mouth to mouth: *self-denial*'. The same point (14.4.), then, might be made by saying that Jesus 'denied himself'.

14.42. 'Death' is an apt metaphor also for the kind of life that Paul recommends for the members of the movement that arose out of Jesus' career, out of, one might say, his 'curriculum mortis'.

14.43. But should there be no 'rapture', no seizure from the sky (1 Thess.4.17 'then we who are alive, who are left, shall be caught up together with them in the clouds to meet the Lord in the air'), the members of the movement can themselves expect to die. 'Death' is already theirs by choice and death is already theirs by prolepsis.

14.44. Thus Christians, literally (they anticipate that they will die) and metaphorically (they have already 'died' <sc. they do not 'please themselves', they 'deny themselves'>), are doubly linked to Jesus. Mutatis mutandis, what is true of the one is true of the others: 'one has died for all; therefore all have died' (2 Cor.5:14).

14.45. And if one is 'alive' for all; therefore all are 'alive'. If 'death' and death can be undergone and survived once, it can be twice. Ab esse ad posse valet consequentia. Life is a structural feature of the universe. Alive now, they now anticipate that they will 'live'; and they are 'alive' now in the sense of being, before death, 'alive' after 'death'. For, confusingly, 'death' is not only an apt metaphor for self-denial (14.41.); it is also an apt metaphor for the life of the man who refuses to deny himself: 'when the commandment came, sin revived and I died' (Rom.8:9).

14.46. To return to the 'gift' model, it may be said: that the 'gifts' Jesus gave were 'death' and 'life' before death and 'life' and 'death' after it; or (and surely with less pointilliste obnubilation: there are too many inverted commas) life not for oneself, but for others, now and in the foreseeable future.

14.47. But if 'gift' is but one model of what is, after all, 'multi-model discourse' (Ramsey, passim), other models from a nexus of models are soon involved. Which is easier to say, 'I have been given a gift' or 'the breath I breath is the breath with which I am inspired' (or 'the intelligence and effectiveness I display are not my own', for 'What have you that you did not receive?' <1 Cor.4:7>).

14.5. Paul is concerned with a number of transitions, such as the passage from metaphorical 'death' to metaphorical 'life'; and the passage from literal death to the 'life' that arises out of death.

14.51. One could speak of a change of mind; or an alteration of mind-set; or the move from the expression of one kind of a symbolic world to another.

14.6. A society that is preoccupied with law will give law a central place in its symbolic world. This is how Paul makes sense of Judaism.

14.7. The 'system of convictions' (Patte, 1983, p.16) to which Paul moved is often called 'Christianity'.

14.71. To make a distinction between 'Judaism' and 'Christianity' is perhaps to be clearer about Paul's situation than Paul was himself. And that perhaps is no bad thing.

14.72. But it is possible that the distinction between 'Judaism' and 'Christianity' does not clarify what is unclear, but represents Paul's situation falsely. For whatever else he also says, he speaks (Gal.6:16) of the new movement of which he has become a vocal or literarily (sc. *letter*arily) polyphiloprogenitive member (it would have been simpler to say that Paul, however much he spoke, wrote more letters than Peter ⟨if less than Cicero⟩) as 'the Israel of God' (Gal.6:16). Pauline Christianity is a version of Judaism.

14.73. Thus we have the choice of speaking perhaps misleadingly of Paul's transition from Judaism to Christianity or perhaps more accurately, and more tiresomely, of his transition from Judaism I to Judaism II or, more baldly and abstractly, from one symbolic system to another.

14.8. It is argued (Sanders, 1977) that in making sense of the symbolic system from which he is in lesser or greater measure departing Paul is not departing from a society in which law is the only thing that occupies the central place. According to this schema, 'law' is joined by 'covenant'. The centre is dyadic, is 'covenantal nomism' (Sanders *op. cit.*).

14.81. Even if Heraclitus would ask us whether you can ever step into the same word twice; even if words 'slip and slide', develop in the course of this 'adventure of divine love' (Tennant, 1930, p.259), alter themselves by 'stepwise adaptation' (Ross, 1981), let us say that the image 'covenant' is political: '... and there was peace between Hiram and Solomon; and the two of them made a treaty' (1 Kg.5:12).

14.82. What part Melkart or Jehovah or any other deities may have played in this arrangement between Hiram and Solomon is not to my purpose.

14.83. What *is* to my purpose is to enquire what the word means when it is used not of a political arrangement between two men who undertake to abide by certain clauses, but what it means when it is used to represent the relations between God and men or God and man. What is its use as an image? What is not its geopolitical, but its '*theo*-political' use?

14.84. When God makes a treaty with man, he undertakes certain treaty obligations. When man takes a treaty with God, he undertakes no treaty obligations. Man merely has to note (and he will note it with satisfaction) that God is taking a burden onto his own shoulders.

14.85. But the two notions, 'covenant' and 'law', can, if you like, be conjoined: God undertakes to do (a), (b) and (c), etc., and man undertakes to do (i), (ii) and (iii), etc.

14.86. Paul is not much intersted in this latter notion. There is an ineluctable 'element of antinomianism' in his thinking (Mackinnon, 1963, p.16). Paul does not combine 'covenant' and 'law'; he distinguishes between them and separates them (Burton, 1921, pp.443 ff).

14.9. Paul is convinced that the small print attached to the treaty that God makes with man applies to the former and not to the latter.

14.91. Better: Paul is convinced that the small print, *if any* ...

14.92. Better still: Paul is convinced that there is *no* small print.

14.93. But (in this vein: Fergusson *obiter scriptum*), if the God of Hiram and Solomon, Abraham and Cain, is not a constitutional lawyer who drafts clauses, is he any more an assessor, accountant or valuator? '... it was *'reckoned'* to him as righteousness (Rom.4:5). Analytically, by definition, God does not 'reckon'; God is uncritical. Much as God may be the subject of the verb 'choose', if the object is 'everybody', so he may be the subject of the verb 'reckon', when the verb means an act of *anagnorisis*, 'recognition', 'acceptance' even (to use Tillich's word), but not an assessment of debit or credit for inclusion in a balance sheet. When theologians choose a verb, it means what they choose it to mean?

14.94. Or is this true of my God, but not of Paul's God?

14.95. To speak of 'covenant' in this way is to give what is at least a partial explanation of the 'system of convictions' (14.7.) to which Paul moved. 'Covenant' is for Paul a central image in a way that 'law' is not: 'you are not under law, but under grace' (Rom.6:14).

15.1. Paul has a quarrel with Jewish rules, because he thinks them inappropriate for non-Jews. He has nothing against circumcision for those who like it, for those who have no objection to tattooing themselves in order to indicate to themselves and to others that their convictions are of one kind and not of another. But he deemed the amputation too drastic to be universalizable: Washing? Yes. Cutting? No. It is not surprising that his opponents accused him of watering down what is required of a relation with God: 'am I trying to please men?' (Gal.1:10). His opponents would not have been at a loss to find an answer to the question.

15.11. Nowadays among the Gentile sections of the Western democracies, 'circumcision' is not a theological issue. Circumcision is something I go to my doctor about; it is not something I go to my priest about. In order to understand the practice, we must either interrogate those who do it as a constituent feature of their relation with God or exercise our historical imagination on texts that speak of it.

15.12. Others have done it. Let others do it.

15.2. Paul has a quarrel also with the food laws.

15.21. This quarrel emerges classically at Antioch (Gal.2:11 ff). Lev.11 specifies a number of animals that may not be eaten. Among these is the camel (v.4). It would be nice to suppose that the trouble arose when the camels on which the Jerusalem contingent had travelled were eaten on arrival by Paul's converts, avid for more than words.

15.3. Paul is content to break the law.

15.31. It is true that what Paul called 'law' covers not only civil law, criminal law and canon law, but also what we call morality and convention. But the case for saying that Paul broke the law is not much thereby weakened.

15.32. At any rate he was subjected to the penalties of the law. By the time of writing 2 Cor.11:24 he could say: 'Five times I have received at the hands of the Jews the forty lashes save one'. Kamlah (1963) tells us what that actually involved.

15.33. But Paul claims that all his actions are responses to the actions upon himself of Jesus of Nazareth. In so far as Paul was a criminal, he was so, aided and abetted by Jesus. He was incited by Jesus to criminal acts. Jesus, qua pre- and post-mortem agent, is the indirect agent of Paul's actions; it is Jesus that causes Paul to act.

15.34. If 'crime' is a forensic analogue of 'sin' (3.12.), then Paul's question, 'Is Christ then an agent of sin?' (Gal.2:17) is equivalent to the question, 'Is Christ then a criminal?'. Paul's question is rhetorical; what his opponents no doubt said was not a rhetorical answer, though it may, one thinks, have had style.

15.4. If you have a code, you can determine who breaks it. A book of statutes is a crime-spotter's manual.

15.41. The Pharisees, or some of them, had a book of this kind that they could not lay down; but it was a book that, with some qualifications perhaps, Paul (nor Jesus for that matter) could not pick up.

15.42. 'Not an iota, not a dot ...' writes Matthew (5:18) and it is probably Paul he is getting at: 'It may well be thought that we have here a reflection ... of the deep suspicion with which Paul was regarded by the more extreme Jewish Christians' (Manson, 1949, p.25).

15.43. 'Not an iota, not a dot ...' says Matthew's Jesus, but 'it is in the last degree unlikely that he thought or said such a thing' (op. cit., p.154 <admittedly re Mt.5:19>). Indeed, it is highly likely that, while saying this or something like it, he meant the opposite: 'I venture to think, that the saying (Lk.16:17 // Mt.5:18) was originally ironical: it was a comment, not on the eternity of the provisions of the Law, but on the obstinate conservatism of the Scribes' (op. cit. p.25). If Marx turned Hegel upside down, Matthew here has up-ended Jesus. He has picked up the stick, but by the wrong end.

15.44. Paul speaks of 'the law of Christ' (Gal.6:2, cf. 1 Cor.9:21). Has Paul access to a law that over-rides the law? Or has he access to something to which legal categories are inappropriate?

15.45. Is it that Paul thinks that law is an inadequate guide to life, that 'everything flows' (Heraclitus) faster than the lawyer or the casuist can determine, that 'anyone who ask(s) for rules, in order to obtain from them instruction how to act, (is) clinging to the lowgrade morality of custom and precept' (Collingwood, 1944, p.73)?

15.46. Paul's 'law of Christ' is an ad hoc formulation, is a forensic phrase with a non-forensic meaning, is a theological sophomore's oxymoron: legal language in theology is in the last resort inept; it is a kind of a debasing of the currency of the like of which Diogenes was accused.

15.47. The Christian man is blown by the wind, when the wind is God's.

15.48. The Christian theologian is a thinking reed, shaken in the wind, when the wind is God's.

15.49. And God's wind can be distinguished from other winds by guess and by God.

15.5. Which is as much as to say that there is a lot that the theologian can get away with: he deems his lies God's truths.

15.6. God is to be 'worshipped', but is to be distinguished from 'His Worship, the Mayor'. 'Mayor' may be an apt model for God, but the model is to be qualified: God is the mayor of mayors;

indeed, the *maximus*. For if the mayor of the town is *maior* (greater) than his fellow-citizens, how much greater, we may suppose, is God. In this instance we move not a *minori ad maius*, 'from the lesser to the greater', but a *maiori ad maximum*, 'from the greater to the greatest'.

15.61. To 'worship' is to acknowledge the worth of someone.

15.62. Worth may be acknowledged by words or by actions that speak louder than or as loud as words.

15.63. Both words and actions may take a regular form. They may form part of a 'rite' or 'cult'.

15.64. And here 'condensation' and 'abbreviation' (5.9.) are at their height. What is abbreviated or condensed is Christianity.

15.7. Those who acknowledge God's worth may be marked for life as by 'circumcision'.

15.71. Or they may be washed for life as by 'baptism': they make the transition from being dirty to being clean.

15.72. It would be wrong to hold that Paul suggests that Christians are not so much cleaned as drowned, but it would be right to say that he is less interested in the transition from being dirty to being clean than in the transition from being alive to being dead. In the context of Rom.6, 'Do you not know that all of us who have been baptized into Christ Jesus ...' (v.6; and so on) 'death' is dominant, 'washing' sub-dominant or, better, dominated.

15.73. (It is astonishing how strongly dominated by the language used of Jesus by Paul is the language used of Paul by Paul.)

15.74. But being 'dead' in the 'baptismal' context of Rom.6 is the metaphorical equivalent of being alive for to be alive and not to be a Christian is best re-described as being 'dead'; and becoming 'dead' is also the metaphorical equivalent of giving up the way of life that is equivalent to being 'dead'. 'Death', that is, has a double reference: (1) to a way of life that should be given up, and (2) to the giving up of that way of life. Paul is an economical writer: why use two terms where one will do?

15.75. But 'death' has yet a further reference: it refers to what happened to Jesus, the man to whom the Christian, as he takes the liminal step, comes to be related, or thinks of himself as coming to be related. And when Jesus was alive, he 'died' in so far as he gave up, renounced alternative modes of being alive; and when he died, that was merely the prelude to coming to be 'alive', of existing in the post-mortem mode, for which 'alive' is an appropriate metaphor.

15.76. There is a plain historical sense of being dead. This plain sense supplies the material for two metaphors: a metaphor for not *really* being alive before you are dead, and a metaphor for making the transition from not *really* being alive to something better, to pre-mortem 'life'. Simultaneously, the plain, historical sense of being dead remains, but being dead in the plain historical sense is succeeded by being 'alive' in a sense that is neither plain nor historical. Only a well-honed machete can take us through this undergrowth of language.

15.77. 'Baptism' is not just nonsense of the first water.

15.8. But 'baptism' in the strict dipping sense, is a very partial experience: a very little water has to stand for very much more.

15.81. Polybius uses the word for 'causing to sink' ships (*Histories*, 1.51.7). But no ship can sink in a font. Moves in the right direction have been made by John the Baptist and the Baptist Union. The relation between 'baptismal' water and the water for sinking or drowning in is synecdochic: the part is standing for the whole, gout for lochan, drop for ocean.

15.82. The water is not for the body; it is for the mind.

15.83. To say that the cleaning is 'spiritual' is the equivalent of saying that it is metaphorical. A medium (water) that is appropriate for cleaning the body is transferred to another semantic field, the mind. After all, we tell a man who swears to 'wash out his mouth'.

15.84. Evil thoughts and actions are like mud. As mud can be washed off, so the mind of an evil agent can be changed.

15.85. It is tempting to pursue the view that Paul supposes Christians to be drowned (15.72.), for he supposes them 'buried'. But the text (Rom.6:3 ff 'Do you not know that all of us who have been baptised into Christ Jesus ...?') shows no sign that that is Paul's view, though there is nothing to stop us from inferring what he did not imply. For burial may as well follow from death by water as from death by crucifixion.

15.9. It was, of course, literally false for Paul to say of the Romans that they were 'buried'. One's correspondence may be 'buried', but not one's correspondents.

15.91. Again (15.83.), to speak of 'spiritual *burial*' is tantamount to speaking of a 'burial' that is metaphorical; but with the added suggestion, if 'spiritual' is a 'craftbound' term, that the undertaker or mourner or officiating person is God.

16.1. To use a metaphor is 'to see x as y' (Nowottny, 1965, p.49): Paul sees living men as dead and buried men.

16.11. Paul sees them so, in part because he remembers that Jesus was, sc. came to be, a dead and buried man.

16.12. By a kind of *glissando*, language proper for the one (Jesus) slides off onto the others (Paul and his companions). There is no detectable break, where language suitable for Jesus comes to an end and language suitable for Paul begins. Discourse about Jesus rubs off onto the others like chalk from a black-board onto a gown. Language proper to the one exercises a kind of imperialism over what is to be said about the others.

16.13. The situation of any man can be conceived as analogous to the situation of Jesus.

16.14. If analogous, then not identical. But the differences are more interesting. Circumstances alter cases and persons alter cases. *Plus ça change, plus c'est une autre chose* ('the more it changes, the more it is a different thing'). And different language will apply. John was unable to be content with Matthew, Mark and Luke; and Katzanzakis with the *Odyssey*.

16.15. But we read Homer and we read Matthew, Mark and Luke. If some sense is to be made of difference and if we are to find some language to express it, we must also make some sense of identity and find our language for that.

16.16. We *stand in a tradition* (if Ebeling <1966> does not say this, he should have done). And if we cannot be content with mere continuity, neither can we be content with mere discontinuity.

16.17. But this view is rather too balanced to deserve credence. To walk is to proceed by a series of imbalances.

16.18. But these remarks (16.1.-16.17.) are too pregnant, imprecise, even if their *nisus* is not in doubt: Paul uses 'Jesus language' (e.g. 'dead', 'buried', 'crucified'); and he uses 'Paul language' (e.g. 'what once had splendour has come to have no splendour at all, because of the splendour that surpasses it' <2 Cor.3:10, thus attacking Hebrew talk>). We may use both, but can be content with neither.

16.2. People speak sometimes of 'union with Christ'.

16.21. Archbishop Makarios had a word for 'union', *henosis*; Paul did not.

16.22. A *'Mothers' Union'* consists of a 'pride' or 'gaggle' of later than nubile women, who are or are supposed to be in sufficient agreement to converse with one another and with any other who ventures to converse with them.

16.23. A *'marital union'* is 'a social contract whereby a man and a woman become partners in the enterprise of producing children ... is conceived as a self-originating status; freely originating itself through the joint act of getting married, and freely maintaining itself through the joint act of living in matrimony. Children are a product of these acts, jointly produced by the two parents ' (Collingwood, 1942, p.162).

16.24. The *'Union of Great Britain and Northern Ireland'* is a political arrangement, to which the English agree.

16.25. A *'union with Christ'* (or a 'mystical union' for that matter) is sometimes a case of 'two walking together', a relation between two individuals, and sometimes the relation between a group, perhaps the whole human group, or perhaps that part of the whole human group formed by the 'Jesus people' or perhaps even 'the whole creation' (Rom.8:22) and the individual, Jesus, to whom they all are or it all is related.

16.3. 'Tell him (sc. James Lenox) that indistinctness is my forte', said Turner, speaking about *Staffa, Fingal's Cave*. The relations between Jesus and Christians in this part of Rom.6 is nothing if not indistinct. Very few capital gains can be made from the prepositions, 'into' and 'with'. A community of life-style may be loosely inferred: both parties, Jesus and the Christians, have found themselves bound to be prepared to be disadvantaged, even annihilated, in their altruistic efforts. And both parties have this in common, that they imagine themselves to be related to God.

16.31. But *deo remoto*, if we may prescind for a moment from God, from the relation of men to God, how is the relation between the man, Jesus, and other men to be specified?

16.32. We must turn elsewhere.

16.33. The relation between Jesus and the Christian is very variously specified. Paul's discourse on the topic is 'multi-model' (14.47.).

16.34. Paul speaks for example of a fraternal union (Rom.8:29 '... in order that he might be the first-born among many brethren') and of a marital union (Rom.7:3 '... if her husband dies ... and she marries another man, she is not an adulteress'). Or it is the union between a 'slave-master' and a 'slave' (1 Cor.7:22 'Likewise he who was free, when he was called, is a slave of Christ').

16.35. What makes a *'mystical* union' mystical?

16.36. The fact that I am fraternally related to my brother does not make that union mystical. But how far is a mystical union to be *peeled*? How far *can* it be? Does a union become mystical if it is with a man who is dead or with a God who is alive?

16.37. More interesting and perhaps more relevant is where Paul speaks of himself in terms of dual personality: '... it is no longer I who live, but Christ who lives in me' (Gal.2:20). Paul's ego is replaced by the ego of Jesus. Paul's ego is not only dominated, but replaced. Tennant's discussion of multiple personality (1928, vol.I, pp.375 f) only moves further along the same road. Another system of sentiments is taking over Paul's normal self. 'Demon-possession *in sensu bono*', we might say; *in sensu bono*, for Paul does not compel us to misconstrue the relation between grace and personality (Oman, 1917); or rather, seeing that Pàul now has *no* personality, the possession is good, because what is possessing is not demonic, but kindly. But *replacement* can hardly be kindly and if there is no longer an ego, there is nothing to possess.

16.38   It might be said that Paul is being rhetorical here, that careless talk has cost him his life, but all that need be said is that in becoming a Christian he was moved from Jonas' (1971) *cogitare me velle* to a *velle me velle*, from, that is, self-conscious reflexion about himself to self-conscious engagement with Jesus. Paul no longer exists for Paul, but that does not mean that he no longer exists for Jesus. He is no longer egocentric, but, at least for the duration of the composition of the sentence he is writing, he is centred on Jesus. He admires; he wonders.

16.4.   But if in dealing with the relation between the Christian and Jesus we are dealing with what can be modelled as fraternal, marital or, in its descriptive, but not in its pejorative sense, servile, we are dealing with a 'brother', a 'husband', a 'slave-master' *'and more'* (Ramsey, *passim*)!

16.41.   This 'brother' is the eldest in the family. This 'husband' was put to death, but 'awoke from sleep'. This 'slave-master' is the 'master of masters': he has 'the name which is above every name' (Phil.2:9).

16.5.   If Paul of Tarsus thought that Jesus of Nazareth was God, he chose an odd way of saying so.

16.51.   He said nothing of the kind,

16.52.   I submit.

16.53.   If a line must be drawn between Jesus and other men, a line must also be drawn between Jesus and God: '... the head of a woman is her husband and the head of Christ is God' (1 Cor. 11:3).

16.54.   But the laywoman will object that if Paul is wrong on the first of these, she providing the feet and he providing the neck, for 'thou hast put all men under her feet' (Ps.8:6), Paul is wrong, too, on the second.

16.55.   Let the laywoman take orders: 'the woman should keep silence' (1 Cor.14:34).

16.6.   If a line can be drawn between Jesus and all other men, a line can be drawn between Jesus and the 'Solon' of the Jews, Moses.

16.61. Paul does not say much about Moses – indeed, he does not say much about anything. According to the evidence at our disposal, he wrote less than Proust or Plato.

16.62. For the life of Moses Paul had access to the biographical legends of the tribe; and possibly too to Philo's *Life of Moses* or to the modes of thought that led to it or from it.

16.63. 'You are looking brighter today', Moses could have been told when he came down from Sinai: 'the skin of his face shone because he had been talking with God' (Ex.34:29). Paul puts it differently: '... the dispensation of death, carved in letters of stone, came with such splendour that the Israelites could not look at Moses' face because of its brightness, *fading as this was*' (2 Cor.3:7; when Paul's sources leave something out, Paul supplies it; if etiolation is required, etiolation is supplied). 'But you won't be looking brighter tomorrow', Paul is saying; 'the light is going out all over Moses'.

16.64. Paul and his sources are making use of 'the symbolism of light in the ancient world' (Bultmann, 1967, pp.323 ff; cf 7.23.).

16.7. Men fear the dark as they fear to go into death.

16.71. If splendour is to be expected in palaces, it may be expected in God's palace: 'light' aligns itself with 'splendour' and 'splendour' aligns itself with empirical monarchies and monarchic imagery: think of something up-market of Solomon.

16.72. 'Light' is a natural apanage of deity. We expect both God and what is said about him to shed light.

16.73. And we expect legislation to shed light on the criminal world. We expect it to dissuade the potential criminal. We expect from it guidance in dealing with criminals.

16.8. If you have a God and something important like law, you will bring the two into conjunction. You will say that God makes it and enforces it, that he (or his officials) is a 'legislator' or 'judge'.

16.81. But, says Paul, the influence of law is deadly. A man who calls law a 'dispensation of death' (2 Cor.3:7) is not mincing his words; he is stewing them as they stand and consuming the result.

16.82. Paul thinks that the legal profession got the wrong man (Jesus).

16.83. And that there is no 'right' man to get.

16.9. But Paul does not use legal criteria to arrive at this view, unless he is saying that Jesus followed the rules he had set himself and that these were in conflict with the rules his society had set for him and that Paul himself is following these same rules.

16.91. Or we can say that Paul used 'more than' (Ramsey again) legal criteria.

16.92. If so, how are 'more than' legal criteria to be specified?

16.93. They may be specified as familial.

16.94. But familial criteria are not criteria at all. Jesus behaved towards his fellow-men as a brother and towards God as a son and there's an end on't: 'Judge not, that you be not judged' (Mt.7:1). 'Have no criteria, if you want to avoid criticism'.

16.95. (Is this position too undialectical? Is there an irreducible tension, polarity between love and justice? 'We must all appear before the judgement seat of Christ' (2 Cor.5:10): does God, does Jesus *both* use criteria, so that we should be left with no illusions (Käsemann, 1980, pp.57 ff) *and* then ignore them?)

17.1. But if you are in a context where legal criteria are *in fact* being implied, even if they should *not* be applied, their application will bring to light the fact that people often behave in a manner that is far from fraternal.

17.11. One is licensed by legal criteria either to acquit or to condemn.

17.12. Time spent in either acquitting or condemning is time lost from fraternal and filial action.

17.13. Jesus is greater than Moses and fraternal and filial action is more important than the application of legal criteria either to oneself or to others, either to acquit or to condemn.

17.2. Lonergan (1972, p.133) distinguishes between theology in direct speech (*in oratione recta*) and indirect speech (*in oratione obliqua*). The examination of Paul's theology is the examination in direct speech of theology in indirect speech: 'Paul said that ...' or 'Paul cursed, namely ...' ('But even if we, or an angel from heaven, should preach to you a gospel contrary to what we preached to you, let him be accursed' <Gal.1:8>).

17.21. To 'curse' is eminently to do theology. A curse has one's personal backing. A curse betrays the 'logic of self-involvement' (to allude to Evans' title <1963>). When a man curses, he is convinced that, or he hopes that his personal backing has God's personal backing.

17.22. Cursing may be performative or optative: 'I curse you', scilicet: 'I hereby reject you, God rejecting you also'; or: 'I wish strongly that you be rejected; and not by me alone, but by God'.

17.23. 'Curse' is a word with an in-built theological component. Not only I am repudiating, God is repudiating.

17.24. But on the assumption that God repudiates no-one, not even his enemies, it is fair to say that what the speaker regards as a performative is regarded by God as an optative. God registers the wish, but does not act on it. Such a wish (to use forensic criteria) is the criminal act of a man, to which God's proper response is acquittal.

17.3. The distinction between direct and indirect speech (17.2.) is easier to draw in theory than to carry out in practice. For we should think rather of the *Ineinanderverflochtenheit* of theory and practice, their mutual implication and complication, their interweaving as a text (Latin: *textum*, 'web'), much as the reader of a letter can become interwoven or inter-mingled (interanimated?) with the text he is reading, for letters can 'mingle souls' (Donne, cit. Gardner, 1982, p.7). And it is often hard to 'un-mingle' the mixture.

17.31. It is not that I write, yet not I, but Paul writes.

17.32. We write.

17.33. Or he wrote and I write.

17.34. For if the interpretation of these classical texts is an adult task that, if it does not demand not less than everything, (though it is *nearly* that, if these texts are classical texts of the kind that they are — but *what* kind is that?) demands a great deal, there is no requirement that the reader succumb to what is written. If the interpretation of these texts 'begins with hearing' (Käsemann *obiter dictum*) it ends or it goes on with our replying, with our arguments, with our objections.

17.35. Conversation is a proper analogy for interpretation and conversation, whatever else it includes, must contain at least my unspoken objections.

17.4. Not only does God 'curse' the opposition in Northern, Central or Southern Turkey, he notes that Jesus has 'become a curse': 'Christ redeemed us from the curse of the law, having become a curse for us' (Gal.3:13).

17.41. A society that makes away with one of its members is rejecting that member.

17.42. A theocratic society, a society whose monarch is God, that makes away with one of its members, can say that that member is rejected by God.

17.43. A critic of such a society will say that that society's rejection is not backed by God's rejection.

17.44. Jesus was condemned by due processes of law. But Jesus was innocent. Therefore the law was an ass.

17.45. Or if the processes were not 'due', the lawyers were asses.

17.5. God accepted the one whom his society rejected.

17.51. You cannot take further measures against someone whom you have annihilated. A dead man is a non-person. Law is now powerless. The lawyers can do nothing more: 'When a man is dead he is free from the law and the commandments' (Sanday and Headlam, 1902, p.159). 'For he who has died has been freed from sin' (Rom.6:7). Legal claims rest when you have a corpse on your hands. The idea was 'a familiar among the Rabbis' (Black, 1973, ad loc.).

17.52. Qua dead, Jesus cannot be got at.

17.53. And if Christians are dead, they cannot be got at either.

17.54. Christians are not only connected to a dead man. They are dead men (this is the metaphorical sense of the verb 'to be').

17.55. The curse that Paul notes (Gal.3:13 '... having become a curse for us') is neither Paul's nor God's. It is the curse of some combination of Jews and Romans and of any supporter of that combination. Paul denies that the word has a proper use here.

17.6. Paul has a system of co-ordinates. The furniture of his mind is stored in a particular room. He has a philosophy, a Weltanschauung, a blik, a perspective. His imagination moves within a symbolic universe.

17.61. Paul's system of co-ordinates, in the argot of the Guild, is 'apocalyptic eschatology'.

17.62. 'Apocalypse' means that the curtains are opened to allow a view; 'eschatology' that the view is a view of the future.

17.63. Paul is a man to whom insights occur, insights into the future: 'It occurs to Paul that ...'.

17.7. It occurs to Paul in Romans 8:21 that he will be free: '... the creation itself will be set free from its bondage to decay and obtain the glorious liberty of the children of God'. A fluoridation programme has been set in train.

17.71. The future Paul envisages has already its anchorage in the present. In some places there are signs of change. For instance, some of the groups that have sprung up have found their 'administrators' (1 Cor.12:28), surely a terminal sign.

17.72. These changes are significant.

17.8. History may be divided in many ways: into the Age of the Wheel, say, or the Elizabethan Age; or some such.

17.81. Paul divides all history into two parts, into the period before Jesus and the period after him. To name the first Paul chooses a fictional character, Adam; to name the second a historical personage, Jesus.

17.82. Whether when he refers to a character from Hebrew fiction, that is what Paul thinks he is doing is a question that I prefer to leave unanswered. Whether or not he thinks he is doing it, he is doing it nonetheless.

17.83. In Romans 5:12-21 Paul speaks of 'Adam' and 'Christ'. Whitehead (1926, p.47) speaks analogously (but not fictionally): 'It (sc. the life of Christ) has the decisiveness of a supreme ideal, and that is why the history of the world divides at this point of time'.

17.9. With the life of Jesus there occurs a caesura: 'the old order changeth, yielding place to new' (Tennyson, *The Passing of Arthur*).

17.91. We move from the realm of history that has been made, the age of Adam, to a realm where history can be made, the age of Jesus; from history made to the making of history.

17.92. We move from the actual to the possible. But more than possible: not only *can* the possible which we now envisage become actual, it *will* become actual.

17.93. What is possible is all that is good. It is all that is good that will become actual.

18.1. But this utopia is infested by primitive survivors of the outmoded system: Paul's ship still sinks (2 Cor.11:25 'a night and a day I have been adrift at sea'); he cannot sleep at night (2 Cor. 11:27 '... through many sleepless night ...'): 'and we know that the whole creation has been groaning in travail together until now' (Rom.8:22). You can count your chickens, but they are not hatched.

18.11. But why should this millenarian dream be infested merely and not destroyed? Why should this oneiric hypothesis not be only apparently veridical, but not really true? What makes it likely that we shall be 'more than conquerors' (Rom.8:37)?

18.12. God or nothing. 'M. Loisy raised his arms and declared, with great deliberation and solemnity, that of course he believed in 'le Grand Mystère'' (Vidler, 1970, p.10). This 'Grand Mystery' is founded on nothing or on God, unless the fact of thirst proves the existence of water. We either 'absolutely presuppose' (Collingwood, 1940) the fact that the world exists or that God is that which explains and cannot be explained.

18.13. But not founded on nothing, surely. There is some evidence for Paul's position, is there not?

18.14. If it is true that 'we hope for what we do not see' (Rom.8:25), it is not entirely true that there is nothing to be seen that would lead us to hope for it. For when Paul was in Thessalonika he twice got hard cash from Philippi (Phil.4:16 'for even in Thessalonica you sent me help once and again'). And more evidence of a similar kind can probably be inferred from the 'healers, helpers' of 1 Cor.12:28.

18.15. More characteristically, Paul appeals either to evidence of an *unlike* kind, to Jesus' misfortunes and his own, or else to evidence of a *like* kind, *where that evidence is intangible*, as to the 'resurrection' and to his own conviction, to his own becoming convinced that 'Jesus was raised' (1 Cor.15:4). But this is evidence that would not survive either a court of law or a historian's judgement.

18.2. Among the topics of theology are God, the universe and what the universe includes. The scope is not mean, even allowing for 'the tin-pot universe of Graeco-Roman antiquity' (Henderson, *obiter dictum*).

18.21. The scope of the Christian's possessions is not mean either: 'All things are yours', says Paul to the Corinthians (1 Cor.3:21).

18.22. The adjective 'all' (in the English) or the noun 'all things' (in Paul's Greek) lends a certain unmanageability to the theological task.

18.23. When Paul says, 'All things are yours', he means what he says. This is proved by the modest catena that follows, as it includes, to name no more, 'the world', 'life' and 'death'.

18.24. When a combination of would-be careful reading and would-be reasonable conjecture is applied to the fissiparous context of the quarrelsome Corinthians to which Paul is referring, it may be added that the views of Peter and Apollos are to be taken with as little seriousness as the views of the author himself. Theology is not only about everything; it is about having a certain attitude to everything.

18.25. What is the logical status of the view that no view is to be taken seriously? Are we to say that no view is to be taken seriously except the view that no view is to be taken seriously?

18.26. 'Give me a place to stand on', Archimedes boasted, 'and I will move the earth'. Paul is convinced that he has been given such a point.

18.3. Käsemann (1980, p.23) begins his preliminary observations on the little word 'faith' in Romans with the observation that it means: 'receive the gospel'.

18.31. And what is a 'gospel' about? It is about Jesus, of course; and about God, of course; and about everything, of course.

18.32. Paul is convinced that everything will come out all right.

18.33. But in the context of the Roman letter we may specify: a gospel, or Paul's version of it, is about God and all men, without regard to questions of race or nationality.

18.4. In 1 Cor.15:24 ff, Paul declares Jesus to be the king's regent. For the time being Jesus is exercising a delegated authority. But there will be a hand-over; power will be transferred back to where it properly belongs, 'that God may be everything to every one' (v.28). With the use of the word 'all' or 'everything' language, as it were, spins off on a drunken orbit. If 'bad company ruins good morals' (Menander, *Thais*, cit. Paul in 1 Cor.15:33), the company of God ruins all discipline of language. It is a characteristic of theological language that it goes 'beyond itself' (Ricoeur, 1978, p.249). Do we need, have we got a grammar of ecstasy, for the place where 'discourse prefers to obliterate itself, to die, at the confines of the being-said' (Ricoeur, *ibid.*)?

18.41. In the context of 1 Cor.15:28 ('When all things are subjected to him ...') a warrior God is fighting the war to end all wars and will win, a sentence that only makes sense when the grammatical subject is God. The indirect agency of God through Jesus will be exchanged for the direct agency of God.

18.42. And why does Paul here resort to military imagery? The symbolic system he is expounding is expounded in the light of the symbolic systems or sub-systems he inherits (in Canaanite mythology, El <God> has a conflict with Mot <Death> <Gibson, 1979>). Paul is not here complaining of the anfractuosities of sublunary travel, or the synagogue and its feral discipline (2 Cor.11:23 ff 'Five times I have received at the hands of the Jews ... on frequent journeys ...'), he is protesting against biological collapse, against the reduction of his 'bone' (sc. 'self', a Hebrew equation) to 'dry bones'.

18.43. To specify in this way one component of the word 'all' (sc. 'El will defeat Mot' or 'we will survive all our difficulties, loss of life included') is not to specify all that might have been specified. To specify one thing is only not to specify nothing, but not to imply that nothing more could be specified.

18.5. The frequency of the word 'word' in Lutheran Protestantism is no less mysterious to me than the imperviousness of the Anglo-Saxon world to deconstruction.

18.51. The notion on the lips of a speaker or from the pen of a writer that God speaks ('God's word' <2 Cor.2:17>) is not surprising. It is not surprising that those who themselves communicate should use in theology a communication model.

18.52. The question, what is modelled by a model, can in theology only be an invitation to supply the questioner with further models. What is modelled by the word of a speaker is the caress or cuff of a father, the reprimand of a judge or his dismissal of one's case.

18.53. It is not surprising either that a writer should write that God writes or that Jesus in his post-mortem mode is a writer: '... you show that you are a letter from Christ delivered by us ...' (2 Cor.3:3). Jesus posts; Paul delivers. The model is qualified: this letter is 'written not with ink'; not even with invisible ink. Coruscating, wind-swift, Paul now moves from inscription or dictation to inflation: this letter is 'written ... with the Spirit of the living God'. Paul's metaphor changes the points and the horses.

18.54. A component of what is modelled here can be said: the Corinthians are lively lads. 'It does not happen to every man to get to Corinth' (Horace), but if you get there you will sit up and take notice: a new and vital group has emerged. The postmen stagger under the weight (2 Cor.3:1 '... do we need, as some do, letters of recommendation?'). Letters are 'mingling' some 'souls' (17.3.), if un-mingling others.

18.6. There are two modes of communication, oral and written. And, grammatology tells us, there are two modes of writing: chisel on stone or pen and ink. For from 'stone' (2 Cor.3:3) we may infer chisel and from 'ink' (ibid.) pen.

18.61. (And theo-grammatology adds a third: 'spirit' on 'hearts' ⟨ibid.⟩.)

18.62. With two contrasting types of written communication there may be contrasted two types of community, Israel and the Christian movement; a community interested in law and order and a community intersted in something else or something more than this.

18.63 And how is this 'something else' or 'something more' to be specified?

18.64. If we say that Paul replaces a régime of 'law' with a régime of 'spirit', we should certainly have to investigate 'spirit', even if we did not have to investigate both.

18.65. And if we say that Paul replaces 'covenantal nomism' (sc. Judaism) with 'participationist eschatology' (sc. Christianity: Sanders, 1977), we should not have answered one question, but raised four.

18.7. However that may be, Paul's opponents think that he cannot just waive the rules and Paul thinks that he can.

18.71. Why does Paul think that he can?

18.72. Or why does Paul think that Jesus is greater than Moses? Or why, to put the matter as Paul puts it, has 'what once had splendour ... come to have no splendour at all, because of the splendour that surpasses it' (2 Cor.3.11)?

18.8. It is clear that Paul thinks that men can put their ears beside God's mouth and that they can read God's correspondence; it is clear that God may be modelled as speaker or writer.

18.81. When I say that God writes, I mean either that God dictates, qua Daddy and not qua Nobodaddy, and Jesus puts pen to paper or that God puts pen to paper and Jesus is what he is writing about. The translator, 'a letter *from* Christ' (2 Cor.3:3), is supposing the former. The translator could have said 'a letter *about* Christ'.

18.82. It is further clear that Paul is modelling God in terms of Jesus, not in terms of Moses. 'Lawgiver' is an improper image for God, in so far, of course, as *any* image is proper for God. So God does not write laws, but wind.

18.83. (But, I hear you cry, not only God does that.)

18.84. Paul models God in terms of Jesus: Jesus 'is the likeness of God' (2 Cor.4:4). And what kind of 'likeness' or image or icon is that?

18.85. What indeed (19.4.)?

18.9. Banality is not Paul's forte. His linguistic facility is more prestidigitatory than to be content either with lapidary incision or with pen and ink.

18.91. Paul's God, writes Paul in a spirited piece of writing, writes with spirit; or, in the orthography of orthodoxy, 'with the Spirit of the living God' (2 Cor.3:3). Upper case makes a better case. And, to be fair, the definite article cannot be omitted: God does not write with spirit, but with '*the* spirit'.

19.1. 'Holy spirit' is 'hard' or 'heavy breathing'.

19.11. If 'to part is to die a little', to sneeze is to expire a little. God's loss of breath is our gain. When a man sneezes, we say 'God bless you!' for fear that the loss should become too great. Being animated by God, we do not need his blessing; nor, having enough suranimation of his own, does he need ours. *Amor* (Catullus XLV, 8 f, 17 f), 'who had before sneezed on the left, now sneezed on the right to show his approbation' of the lovers: a sneeze on the left is sinister, on the right all right; but to sneeze at all must be sinister for someone, in this case for *Amor*, for whom exhalation is expense of spirit, though for the lovers who *inhale* inspiriting.

19.12. In the Hebrew bible, which Vermes might have called 'the poacher's pocket-book' (13.35.) of 'the dispensation of condemnation (2 Cor.3:9), the word 'spirit' (Briggs, 1900) runs from the 'north wind' ('The north wind brings forth rain; and a backbiting tongue, angry looks' <Prov.25:23>) to the omnipresence of God ('Whither shall I go from thy Spirit? Or whither shall I flee from thy presence? If I ascend to heaven, thou art there! If I make my bed in Sheol, thou art there!' <Ps.139:7 f>).

19.13. But why 'spirit' and 'presence'? Why not 'breath' and 'face'? 'There are silk clothes in the wardrobe', Aldous Huxley points out, is an anodyne paraphrase of: 'And silken dalliance in the wardrobe lies'. Why paraphrase by prose, translate by abstraction?

19.2. But 'the spirit as that which breathes quickly or hard in animation or agitation of any kind ...' (19.1.) is only the third of Briggs' (1900, p.135) ninefold classification: 'heavy breathing' is not the full story.

19.21. What kind of animation, suranimation was going on in Corinth? And did Paul know? Was it the parted lips of Michelangelo's youths on the Sistine ceiling? Was it such animation, but an animation 'christologised' and 'moralised' (Käsemann, 1980, p.213)? More or less common sense gives us access to morality, but what is 'christologised' animation? The willingness to 'carry in the body the death of Jesus' (2 Cor.4:10)? The preparedness not 'to please ourselves ... For Christ did not please himself ... (Rom.15:1,3)? The kind of vitality that Jesus displayed was the readiness to lose his own?

19.3. All the time I am attempting to make inroads into Paul's imagination.

19.31. It is very clear that Paul is an animated writer. His mind is well 'dunged' with ancient literature and in that soil thus heated (an earlier draft here read 'treated', but machine intelligence, aptly so called, lit on the former, which I now prefer) his imagination flowers. By 'ancient literature' I mean not Menander and the like, chiefly, but the 'pocket-book' of the Jews.

19.32. His mind here in 2 Cor.3 is shown to be a quicksilver mind, darting from point to point like a trout from stone to stone. He produces what we find in Finnegan's Wake, the associative surprises (Fitzmyer, 1981) of the schizophrenic.

19.33. It is clear, in general from his writing clear, that Paul is recommending that the form of life that Jesus adopted for himself be adopted by his correspondents. And Jesus' form of life Paul regards as a fair representation of the form of life that God has adopted for himself. From these indicatives about the life of God and the life of Jesus, in both its pre- and post-mortem mode, follow the imperatives that Paul addresses to his readers: how Jesus was, how God and Jesus were, is how Paul's readers ought to be.

19.34. But it is fair to add again (14.36.) that these imperatives are only a sub-dominant theme. It is *almost* as if concentration on the indicatives is *all* that is required. As Bonhoeffer puts it in the *Ethics* (1983, p.3): 'The knowledge of good and evil seems to be the aim of all ethical reflection. The first task of Christian ethics is to invalidate this knowledge ... Man at his origin knows only one thing: God'.

19.35. In his footnote (1958, p.11 <14.33.>) Wittgenstein need only have said: 'Now this picture can be used (and should be used) ... to tell how a particular man did stand in such-and-such a place'.

19.36. But is the abolition of ethics coherent? It could be said that to know God is to know what God requires and what God requires is what I ought to do. Or could it be said that to know God is to know that which transforms and that that transformation by-passes ethical reflection; and indeed that the knowledge of God can only be impeded by such reflection?

19.4. Paul regards Jesus' form of life as a fair representation of the form of life God has adopted for himself (19.33.). Jesus, in Paul's words, is 'the likeness of God' (2 Cor.4:4).

19.41. 'The story says that' Seth (Collingwood, 1940, p.56 <we are not dealing with history>), born in his father's two hundred and thirtieth year, bore a family resemblance to him (Gen.5:3).

19.42. If we remain within the same genetic or ancestral register, if we stay in this corner of the lexical field, it may be said that Jesus bears a family resemblance to his father.

19.43. Christians, similarly, bear a family resemblance to their father (God) and *a fortiori* to their brother (Jesus).

19.44. With Christians this familial metaphor very quickly breaks down. The resemblance (how is it to be best expressed?) between any Christian and either his brother or father or both is imperfectly discernible. The metaphor of the family may be salvaged by the introduction of 'adoption', thus 'qualifying the model' (Ramsey, *passim*): not 'brother', but 'brother by adoption'. Adopted members will not share the features, but can more or less completely share the values, of the family.

19.5. In 2 Cor.2:14 Paul turns to a doxology: 'But thanks be to God ...'. The macro-text of the letter contains a number of micro-texts; here a doxology or ejaculatory comment on God's brightness.

19.51. Paul is grateful, not to a human group, but to God. He examines God, weighs God in the balance and finds that his scales incline. What Paul is making is an *anagnorisis* or recognition of worth, the worth not of a man, who is greater than his human fellows, but of God who is greater than any fellow you care to mention.

19.52. Is this expression of gratitude haphazard? By what is Paul here motivated? By what is this micro-text prompted?

19.6. Paul has his problems that are not soluble by Paul. If God has his problems, they are problems that he can solve.

19.61. The contrast, to use a military idiom, is between defeat and victory, permanent defeat and permanent victory. There is a general who can make capital out of Paul's setbacks. Behind (before? preveniently before?) the frontline or 'sharp end' there is support for Paul.

19.62. The assertion is bald. Paul's assertion, that he is supported and so is grateful, itself needs support. Or is Paul merely flying in the teeth of the evidence? Is Paul simply an optimist, one who is 'in incomplete possession of the facts' (as the optimist has been defined)?

19.63. But if Paul's assertion, that he has support, is a presupposition and a presupposition that is 'absolute' (18.12.), it is insupportable.

19.7. Distance is required between a reader and a text. It is better to use a crowbar on Paul than to grasp him with one's bare hands.

19.71. Such a gap permits what has been called 'the hermeneutics of creative distortion' (Matheson, 1979).

19.72. I suppose this is to say no more, if no less, than that the present is ineluctably involved in an enquiry into the past.

19.73. In a less green and salad manner, McDonald (1954, p.406) makes the same point (and he is merely doing history; theology compounds the problems): 'Historical reconstruction does not mean drafting a sketch, as it were, in two dimensions, regardless of our own position in the present or the problems of historical knowledge. Our impression of history is three-dimensional. We look back from a distance, down a long historical vista obscured by time and tradition, towards an unfamiliar scene, which we dimly perceive and which we interpret as best we can. By analysis we may reduce the distortion, by study we may clarify the picture, but we cannot remove the intermediate effects'.

9.8. Paul used metaphors. His theology consists of little else.

9.81. 'Metaphor is the dreamwork of language and, like all dream-work, its interpretation reflects as much on the interpreter as on the originator. The interpretation of dreams requires collab-oration between a dreamer and a waker, even if they be the same person; and the act of interpretation is itself a work of the imagination. So too understanding a metaphor is as much a creative endeavour as making a metaphor, and as little guided by rules' (Davidson, 1979, p.29).

9.82. And the tenor of Paul's metaphorical vehicle is itself a dream: 'We shall not all sleep' (1 Cor.15.51). There is an analogy between Paul's view of the future and a dream. Paul's theol-ogy is oneiric (2.52.).

9.83. A dream, not a nightmare. There is an 'essential identity of all human efforts to establish friendly relations with that higher unity of spirit and matter which we speak of as the universe. Go we ever so far back in such historical retrospect as our fragmentary records allow it is always the same picture, as at least I see it, of a creature asserting and achieving dominance, spiritual no less than material, by sole reason of a stupendous optimism' (Marett, 1933, pp.3 f). 'All human efforts' include Paul's. 'Life', not 'death', is Paul's terminal category, 'stupen-dous optimism' his mood.

9.9. To say that Paul makes use of metaphors is to say that he makes use of heuristic fictions.

9.91. What is to be *gained* by saying that Paul makes use of either? Why not rest content with Paul's 'ontological vehemence' (Ricoeur, 1978, p.249) without analysing what ontology is involved?

9.92. By noting the fact, if it *is* a fact, we learn to unravel Paul's text with circumspection. When Paul after a sleepless night eventually fell asleep and woke up, he woke in a different sense from the sense in which Jesus woke after death.

9.93. 'Resurrection' seems to be a term that lexically marks that difference. But, for all that, it says with a Latin root what 'awakening' says with an Old English root *(awaecnan)*. It does not tell us *what* is meant by awakening after a sleepless death, but tells us that *whatever* is meant by awakening after a sleepless death is like awakening after a night of sleep or *is* awakening after a night of sleep in a sense that implies an *is not* awakening.

20.1. That great 'awakening' is one of Paul's root metaphors that carries his theology.

20.11. But is *that* root metaphor no longer 'active' or even 'dormant' but 'extinct' (9.61.)? Has 'resurrection' ceased to redescribe what happens after death as 'awakening' and become an index of what happens after death without picturing what happens then in any way at all? Does 'resurrection' remain volcanic sc. 'active', only as the idea *that* something happens then without providing a picture of *how* it happens, a picture of the transition from sleep to wakefulness? Are we told *that* something happens without being told *how* it happens?

20.12. Paul refuses, of course, to speculate on the comparative anatomy of pre- and post-mortem bodies: 'But some will ask, 'How are the dead raised?' ... You foolish man!' (1 Cor.15.35). Does Paul thereby show that he is aware of the limits of metaphorical thinking, of the metaphorical imagination?

20.13. The root metaphor 'awakening' is not quite extinct; else how would Paul say 'We shall not all sleep' (1 Cor.15.51)? The word 'sleep' occurring in the context of 'awakening' suggests that 'awakening' is thought of in relation to 'sleep' and so does not mean 'transition' *tout court*, but 'transition from sleep'.

20.14. But 'sleep' in 1 Cor.15.51 may *itself* be extinct: in other words a mere synonym for 'death': 'We shall not all sleep' has the same force as 'We shall not all die'. And then, if that is so, it is doubtful whether a dead metaphor, 'awakening', can be resurrected by another, 'sleep', that has no life.

20.15. But 'awakening', it is perhaps not unfair to say, is not extinct if not quite active. 'Awakening' lies dormant for an awakening by some Shakespeare (9.62.).

20.2. The weight of Paul's theology is carried by a half-dead or comatose metaphor?

20.3. Root metaphors, even dormant or half-dead ones, may be distinguished from branch metaphors by the respective weight they carry. God 'is leading a victory parade' (2 Cor.2:14 '...leads us in triumph ...') through the streets of Corinth or Ephesus or Troas or wherever, is subordinate in the hierarchy of metaphors in a way that God's 'justice' or 'acquittal' or 'moral rectitude' is not.

20.31. But 'God is leading a victory parade' can of course be correlated with, is of course coherent with Jesus' 'awakening', if God, in awakening Jesus, can be said to be defeating a person a person who is hostile, just in case that person is to be identified with death. The general is showing he knows how to win a war, is showing he has tactical and strategic sense, when the 'enemy' is 'death' (1 Cor.15.26).

20.4. Are there observation statements to justify these heuristic fictions? What is there to *show* for them?

20.41 What doctor ever detected Paul's quickened pulse? (How do you quantify the energy of an individual or a group?) On how many occasions did Paul approach a travel agent? How low did the hatters' sales-graph fall or by how many women on how many occasions was the yashmak refused (for a woman 'ought to have a veil on her head because of the angels' <1 Cor. 11:10>)? What kind of an index is the occurrence of intemperate, epistolary prose?

20.5. The Jew's conception of justice differs, in Paul's view, from God's conception of it.

20.51. One might as well say, I suppose, that the Jew's conception differs from Paul's conception. At any rate, the second formulation has the merit of greater brevity.

20.52. By human criteria, God's justice should be defined as injustice: he acquits the guilty. It is Pickwickian justice.

20.53. By Paul's criteria, for he shares God's criteria, justice as formulated by Jewish thinkers contains errors. Circumcision, the private tattoo, is not universalisable. The community of which God and men are members ought not to contain only those who have been circumcised. An enumeration of 'the concision' (Phil.3:2 <AV>) is too concise. No such gonfalon need be flown. The community contains rather those who want to be contained by it.

20.54. So far Paul, but an enumeration of less than all men is too mean. The community of God and man contains, though it does not cabin or confine, even those who do not wish to be contained.

20.6. There are two questions that may relevantly be asked concerning justice: How can I be just? and: How is God just? Paul's concentration is without a shadow of doubt on the latter.

20.61. His view of God's activity is that it is such as to inspire with confidence.

20.62. God's activity is patent and pertinent and may very nearly be reduced to, no, can be studied in a concentrated way by studying the activity of Jesus.

20.63. But when Jesus was dead, his activity was reduced to nil. When there is no longer an agent, there cannot be any action.

20.64. Yes, if and only if it is true (so *King Lear*) that *ex nihilo nihil fit*, that 'nothing comes from nothing'. But not everything that stands in a text is valid.

20.65. Then, if for Jesus dead something came of nothing, Paul is permitted to infer the like for Paul. For *ab esse ad posse valet consequentia,* it is reasonable to conclude from a fact a possibility. Or can we only conclude that *that* fact must have been possible, but no other facts of a like kind, that if something came of Jesus dead it was possible that something could have come of him, but not that something *can* come of Paul?

20.7.   Justice is an abstract term. It needs a context if it is to be given flesh and bones. Who is said to be just to whom and on what occasion?

20.71. In Romans 10:9 f, God's justice and Jesus' revivification are mentioned in one breath: '... if you believe in your heart that God raised him from the dead, you will be saved. For man believes with his heart and so is justified ...'.

20.72. Jesus, we might say, is being awarded compensation for damages. In the case where crucifixion is the damage, resurrection is awarded by the court in compensation.

20.73. Or the Wallace, we might say, is fighting to free his countrymen from oppression.

20.74. God's justice, that is, may be conceived forensically (20.72.) or militarily (20.73.).

20.75. In the first case, the Jews, or some of the Jews, are those against whom the case for damages is brought; in the second, they are those who administer an oppressive system of government. (The Jews? *Some* of the Jews only? − *Tua res agitur,* 'it is *you* who are concerned in this, *your* story is being told here'.)

20.76. Does the 'justice' model license this inference about the opponents of justice, or is it 'a fruitless task pressing the metaphor ... in an endeavour to elaborate out of it (a theory of) the atonement' (Black, 1973, p.66)? If Paul thinks in 'film-strips', not in metaphysical propositions (*ibid.*), is such comment on 'the Jews, or some of the Jews' part of the 'film-strip' itself or a legitimate part of the film-critic's concern? How far are Paul's metaphors to be pressed? Are they to be pressed further than Paul pressed them?

20.77. Paul's use of the text, 'Cursed be every one who hangs on a tree' (Deut.21:23; Gal.3:13) suggests that a sense of outraged justice is one of the motive forces of his writing: if God is just and Jesus of Nazareth was a just man, then it follows that the Jews, or some of them, were unjust men. And against the unjust let us cast a stone.

20.78. But Paul thinks, of course, that all men (but Jesus) are unjust, so his inference about some of the Jews contains no necessary arrogance. In the dark all men are grey.

20.79. But on the question whether the Jews or some Jews were defendants or oppressors the line between legitimate inference and unwarranted speculation is blurred. In the dark all cats are grey.

20.8. A storm in a wine-cup at Antioch (Gal.2:11 ff 'But when Cephas came to Antioch, I opposed him to his face ...') prompts Paul to set out on the path of redefining justice.

20.81. The incident was in itself trifling and to the modern or non-Jewish mind almost incomprehensible: whether or not non-Jews too should be persuaded to the *pericope* or vivisection of their private parts. There were those who said 'Yes'; there was Peter who said first 'Yes', then 'No', then 'Yes'; and there was Paul who said 'No', and again 'No'.

20.82. But perhaps it was not so much the pericope or circumcision that was at issue as the wine-cup, the question, who had had his hand on the bottle and what had been in his mind at the time: had it been Dionysus or had it been Jesus or Jesus and his father? Had it been a libation to Jesus or a eucharist to *posis das*, 'the husband of the earth', Poseidon?

20.83. But it is difficult to raise enthusiasm either for either issue or for either side of either.

20.9. Paul is not much concerned with the question, How can I be good?

20.91. Paul seems not to be able to rest content with the view that there exist some laws, which are asinine, but only with the view that the law, the law *tout court*, is an ass.

20.92. And yet the law, Paul also holds, is *not* an ass, for 'You shall love your neighbour as yourself' (Lev.19:18). In this 'one word', sc. in these seven words, 'the whole law is fulfilled' (Gal.5:14).

20.93. 'Perhaps it is not unfair to conclude from the modern studies of these things that any interpretation which arrives at a perfectly coherent picture of the state of his mind is in danger of misleading us' (Griffith, 1954, p.155 <on Herodotus>).

20.94. We may translate 'law' by 'the system of Judaism' and we may say that to the system of Judaism Paul opposes the system of Christianity. But, if we say so, we are also under obligation to say where these systems are different and where they overlap.

20.95. Does the difference lie in being law-abiding on the one hand and in being good on the other? Or even in being legalistic and being legal?

20.96. 'Bagpipes are not susceptible to *midras*-uncleanness' (*Mishnah*, Kelim 20.2 <*midras*: 'place of pressure or treading'>). But even if we do not need to enter upon a discussion of what does not happen to them, but happens to the saddle on which a menstruating woman sits, the broad contrasts between legality and legalism, morality and law remain vacuous until some context is given: *what* is being understood by *what* person in *what* situation?

21.1. What changes people is not how laws are formulated, but how God is or how God acts. More important than the question (if it should be asked at all), 'What ought I to do?' is the question, 'What is it that enables me to do what I ought?'

21.11. The rule that a man ought to love may be unchangeable in its formulation. Not so in its application. It is a rule, one might say, that states nothing. It is not worth the stone it has been chiselled on.

21.2. If Paul is incoherent, one should not work too hard at making him so (20.93.).

21.3. Paul (20.8.) 'redefines justice'.

21.31. The alert, even the inert, reader will have noticed that no very clear account was given either of the definition of justice that Paul inherited or of the definition he produced.

21.32. That is not easily done. All that can be asserted for the moment is that non-Jews need not cut themselves *about* and that those who advocate that they need to can happily cut themselves *off*: 'I wish those who unsettle you would mutilate themselves' (Gal.5:12).

21.33. But along with the view that *one component* (sc. circumcision) of the legal system or system of the Jews is a matter of indifference, 'for neither circumcision counts for anything, nor uncircumcision, but a new creation' (Gal.6:15), there goes, I think, the suggestion that the legal system, the system of the Jews itself, *what the components compose*, can *indifferently* be respected or ignored. God is of the *esse* of religion, the principles and practices of canonical procedure not so.

21.4. None of this quells Paul's paraenetic orgies. He is full of good advice. Each of his letters, usually, contains an ethical section. Indifferent to precepts, he produces them. Busily engaged in sawing off the branch on which he is sitting, he is busily engaged in grafting it on. 'Paul was never slave to consistency; but there are few more brilliant inconsistencies than the letter (1 Corinthians) in which he deals with the disorders which had arisen out of a perfectly logical interpretation of his own teaching' (Knox, 1932, pp.94 f).

21.41. But these ethical sections are ancillary. The account of *God's* activity is primary.

21.5. God's activity is just activity.

21.51. The 'justice' of God is a central metaphor, a 'root paradigm' (Turner and Turner, 1978, p.248) that reaches 'down to the irreducible life stances of individuals, passing beneath conscious prehension to a fiduciary hold on what the individual senses to be axiomatic values, matters literally of life and death' (ibid.).

21.52. God is just, men are unjust; men, all men, are criminals and the judge, God, acquits them.

21.53. The sensory end of the paradigm lies in the forensic procedures of Judaism, in their court-houses, at 'the gate', at the city boundary.

21.54. And in the forensic procedures of Hellenism, in their court-houses (but not at the city boundary).

21.55. Ideologically, the paradigm functions to produce a liminal condition, in which sexual, social and racial status is relaxed: 'there is neither Jew nor Greek ...' (Gal.3:28).

21.6. In Romans 11:5 Paul speaks of 'a remnant chosen by grace'.

21.61. By his use of the term 'choice' Paul shows that he is ignorant of the asymmetrical nature of theological propositions. It does not follow from the assertion, God has chosen me, that he has not chosen you.

21.62. Or vice versa.

21.63. 'Choice' belongs within theological discourse only in the Pickwickian or Barthian (1957, p.306) sense of 'I choose everybody', much as 'love' belongs within it only in the polygamous or pantogamous sense: hieros gamos or marriage when God is the subject, when God is the bridegroom, combines endogamy and exogamy in one.

21.64. It is true that Paul is following the conventional bifurcations of the prophet Malachi: 'I have loved Jacob, but I have hated Esau' (Mal.1:2 f; Rom.9:13). But this is not to save the truth, but to double the error.

21.65. There is a difference between being selected by an executioner and being selected by a suitor.

21.66. If Paul nods, if Paul is content to depict God as 'a non-moral despot' (Dodd, 1932, p.159), it is only fair to say that he goes on later to provide the premises from which the universalist conclusion must be drawn (op. cit., p.184). One finds in Paul what the curate found in his egg.

21.67. These remarks are not 'non-vacuous description' merely, nor 'explanation' merely, but 'evaluation' (Weitz, 1965). They belong to the criticism of Paul as an evaluation of Paul.

21.7. A well-written book is like a rifle, but a scatter-gun may bring down a pheasant.

21.71. After all, the contents of Paul's occasional pieces are very disparate: eating, getting married (or not getting married), shopping ...

21.8. Take: eating.

21.81. Take eating, on its own and along with some associated commonplaces, commonplaces common to Christians.

21.9. We eat now on the ground, to show that we are expecting to eat 'in the air' (1 Thess.4:17). What we shall do, when we will be with God, may be modelled as a meal.

21.91. To speak politically, we are allies with God. We are allies *of* God. God's relation with man, or GrM (where G is God, r is relation ...) may be modelled as an alliance. We make it, we enter into it, we draw it up, we sign it, and the like. For this is the burden, the purport of 'covenant' in 2 Cor.3:6.

22.92. Historically, we recall Jesus' execution. We remember it, we have evidence for it, 'the evidence at our disposal allows us to conclude that ...' (Collingwood, 1940, p.56).

22.93. Jesus, metaphorically, was an animal, slaughtered and burnt. We complexify history stereosophically. Our 'vision' is 'stereoscopic' (Stanford, 1936, p.105), is synoptic, synoptic of the practice of government, of what on one occasion was practised by one particular government, and of regular behaviour with animals, when animals are food for the gods, for gods and men.

22.94. There is a neat correlation between bread and body on the one side and wine and blood on the other. The notions of feasting and execution inter-penetrate.

23.1. 'The story says that ...' (12.51.) the Jews on the way from Egypt to Israel found food supplies (1 Cor.10:3 'all ate the same supernatural food').

23.11. It is said of Henry James, not that he bit off more than he could chew, but that he chewed more than he bit off: minds need food like bodies do, need something to chew on.

23.12. Moreover, if anyone has ever become free of slavery, it may be that others can become so. What has happened once, can happen again.

23.2. The Jews found food (23.1.) *and* water. And, say it how you please, they kept finding water — or the water kept finding

them, it followed them about: 'they drank from the supernatural Rock which followed them' (1 Cor.10:4).

23.21. Jewish thought is not without its *jeux d'esprit*. Did not Adam,
'extending from one end of the earth to the other, and from
heaven to earth', get reduced at the Fall to a hundred yards
(Davies, 1948, p.45)? Even after his Fall Adam could have
taken a world record in his stride.

23.3. Paul's account of the Christian Mass is *inter alia* a compound
of 'alimentary symbolism' (Marett, 1933, p.22) and historical
memory.

23.31. A man may be grateful for being nourished in body and mind.
'Eucharist' in Greek has to do with being grateful. For if
'<h>unger is, at any rate in part, a certain group of *feelings*;
for example, a 'gnawing' sensation at the stomach, a general
organic sensation of weakness or lassitude, with an inability to
see clearly and a tendency for things to go black, and an emo-
tional feeling of gloom or depression' (Collingwood, 1942,
p.15), then satified hunger is a bodily pleasure and one who is
bodily pleased is properly grateful.

23.32. In the hocus-pocus of the Eucharist the mind is nourished by
remembering what Jesus did and what happened to him. For
something like what has happened once can happen again.

23.33. But what is remembered is very nearly reduced to the remembering that he died. But Jesus' death stands by synecdoche
(14.33.) for his life.

23.34. What did Jesus live for?

23.35. 'He was for others' (Bonhoeffer, 1959, p.165)? He instantiated
benevolence (6.34.)?

23.36. Let the question stand.

23.37. What is remembered is very nearly reduced to Jesus' death.

23.4. But not quite. For Jesus is said to have said: 'This is my
body ...' (1 Cor.11.24).

23.41. A man may eat a loaf of bread, but if more than one man is
to eat it, the loaf has to be divided into pieces. Similarly, if
any one man is to nourish his fellows, he will find it 'under the
conditions of existence' (Tillich, *passim*) an expensive business.

23.42. 'This cup is the new covenant ...' (1 Cor.11:25). Alliances, too,
can be costly. Not all those who fight for them live to make
them; and not all those who live to make them can make them
without the struggle to deracinate the rooted prejudices that
would prevent them.

23.5. If Paul says (1 Cor.11:26): '... as often as you eat ... you pro-
claim the Lord's death until he comes', the implication is that

the Lord is not there. This is Paul's doctrine of the 'Real Absence'.

23.6.   There is an analogy between the way Gödel's theorem relates to a physical determinate system and the way Paul's views relate to the system of Judaism (and any theological system that diverges from Paul's own?). God does not belong within the system of theology, though the system of theology is dependent on him.

23.7.   My aim is to de-stabilise the language that we use to speak of Paul. 'Change the currency!' Ecrasez l'infâme!

23.8.   Paul is not strong on marriage.

23.81. To other reasons, some of which can be cited, for avoiding wholly matrimony, Paul adduces the purposes of God, frenetically construed.

23.82. Indeed, the mind of Paul's God has the mind of a first century Hellenistic Jew, whose identity can be more nearly specified:

23.83. Paul.

23.84. But what theologian has ever attributed to his God a mind that differed from his own? Paul's 'identikit' of God is Paul's twin.

23.85. The married man, Paul adds, is compelled to consider his wife: 'the married man is anxious about worldly affairs, how to please his wife' (1 Cor.7:33). And the interests of one's wife do not, perhaps cannot, co-incide with the interests of God.

23.86. No-one who has immersed himself in or been submerged by worldly affairs of this kind and their implicate, offspring or 'offsprings' (Gal.3:15), can deny that Paul's admonition is without some force. But (to 'evaluate' <21.67.>) the disjunction is alarming and must, by an easy descent along the primrose path of over-eager religion, lead down to stipulatory bachelorship. If the world is not to end 'before the corn is ripe' (the phrase, I think, is Schweitzer's <1911>), the practice must soon culminate in a dearth of initiates to drown.

23.87. But to be fair, Paul is diffident: '... concerning the unmarried, I have no command of the Lord ...' (1 Cor.7:25). The mind of Jesus and the mind of God may not perfectly co-incide with Paul's own. Though, to be fair on the other side, Paul's diffidence does not quench his speech. No-one may have told him to think it, but he thinks it nonetheless: 'I say this ... to secure your undivided devotion to the Lord' (1 Cor.7:35). But what if one's wife is one's neighbour? Or what if the girl next door was one's neighbour? Whom one was bound to love as oneself?

23.9. Paul's views on sexual questions are reluctant and regulatory.

23.91. There are sexual questions on which Paul has no view at all (10.51.). Indeed, eros, toxophilite, finds no major treatment in the combined documents of the old and new alliance except as a metaphor for God's relation with man: 'Your teeth are like a flock of shorn ewes that have come up from the washing, all of which bear twins ...' (Song 4:2). Or did the secularists get it past the authorities in a theological cover? Was the literal sold as metaphor?

23.92. There are sexual prejudices that Paul shares with the majority of his countrymen: there is a hierarchy which has God at the top and woman at the bottom. Along with 'garlic and sapphires' (Eliot, *The four Quartets*) woman lies in the mud. And 'clot the bedded axle-tree' (*ibid.*).

23.93. We must turn elsewhere for an adequate treatment of these matters. 'Until the day breathes and the shadows flee (we must) hie (us) to the mountain of myrrh' (Song 4:6).

23.94. Sexual activity, by Paul's and God's lights, is closely correlated with idolatry.

23.95. Both may have a point to make.

23.96. Idolatry is *another* man's theology.

24.1. It is Paul's view that one man's god is another man's devil, but that one man's meat is another man's meat. He allows his progressive views on butcher-meat to be blackmailed by the stick-in-the-muds.

24.11. 'As Zimmern has said, the usual Attic dinner consisted of two courses, the first a kind of porridge, and the second a kind of porridge' (Kitto, 1951, p.33, cit. Barrett, 1964-5, p. 145). With a little bit of luck, the question of 'The Sunday Joint of the Christian Housewife' (Ehrhardt, 1964, pp.276 ff) would never have arisen.

24.12. But it did. Not only might one find oneself dining with the french-Beytaghs, to keep up with the Smiths, but supping at the sofa of Sarapis (Deissmann, 1927, p.351, fn.2, cit.Barrett, *op. cit.*, p.146). And meat is not only meat if it is declared to be more than merely Smiths' meat.

24.2. If there is any sense in God's godhead, as we suppose in presupposing that a theology is to be judged by moral criteria, there must be a sense in which God's perspective from that other country allows him to be earlier involved in our grief than we are ourselves. The involvement is earlier because, from that better perspective, he can see the way things are developing.

24.21. It is Paul's view that God comforts. He speaks (2 Cor.1:3 f) of the 'God of all comfort, who comforts us in all our affliction so that we may be able to comfort those who are in any affliction, with the comfort with which we ourselves are comforted by God'. The paronymic anaphora is five-fold.

24.22. The transition from needing comfort to getting it is analogous to being dead and coming to life.

24.23. Paul's 'stupendous optimism' (19.83.) is grounded in nothing, if not in God, though we need hardly suppose that Paul was always without other allies: Timothy, for instance (2 Cor.1:1).

24.24. The word 'all' in the 'God of all comfort' is a qualifier that characterises theology. There may have been gaps in the cheerfulness of Timothy, but indefectibility is the watchword here. Else a greater could be conceived. A religion is not a religion if there remains a negative which cannot 'somehow' (the word is Mackinnon's word) be converted to a positive; if (may we say?) it can be falsified. The word 'all', as Bultmann points out (1976, p.26) converts secular to religious language or at any rate is a feature of 'liturgical style'.

24.25. Paul tells us he is referring, while *also* referring to *everything*, to *one* thing in particular that happened to him in the west of Turkey. He does not satisfy our curiosity by telling us what it was. Perhaps he is referring to his interruption of the Ephesian trinket trade run on Artemis' behalf by Demetrius the silversmith (Ac.19:23 - 20:1). But Paul is less interested in the circumstances he was in than in the fact that the property of fortitude is 'absolutely presupposed' (18.12.), or that fortitude is the effect of a 'cause' (11.55.) and the 'cause' is God: there is that than which there is nothing better to keep us all going, which some call Artemis and others not. For some prefer the Ortygian polymast and some the Hebrew polymath.

24.3. Paul's initial insight was that Jesus' reformist views were not in error, but that a world religion that demanded surgery as the price of admission was not likely to be a winner.

24.4. It may well be that Paul spent some of his time at Corinth making tents for the spectators of the Isthmian games (Broneer, 1962).

24.41. It may well be that he did not.

24.42. Perhaps his tents went to Olympia, Nemea, or Delphi. And none without its tract.

24.43. It is, of course, possible to sew and talk at the same time; to sew and to sow at the same time Christian seeds, (1 Cor.9:11 'If we have sown spiritual good among you ...').

24.5. The student of Paul has to learn when he can no longer ask questions usefully of him. He has to learn when to be content with the observation, 'Well, that is what Paul thinks'. But much of importance depends on the just estimation of when that point is reached and from what direction.

24.6. The Christian religion, for Paul, is a device for breaking rules.

24.7. Christians, in Paul's view, die not from terminal, but from liminal illness.

24.8. It is likely that the same medicine that Paul had earlier offered the Christians was offered to Paul the Christian by the Jews. 'Paul the Christian' here is equivalent to 'Paul the deviant Jew' and by 'Jews' not 'the Jews' *simpliciter*, but 'the Jews in charge'. It is not always possible to break the law with impunity or abet with impunity the criminal activity of others. And if you do it *Chresto impulsore*, 'at the instigation of Christ', you do no more than show that Jesus was a criminal; you do no more than confirm the verdict of Pilate's court. That is not, of course, to say that the reasons why Pilate punished Jesus co-incide with the reasons why the synagogue disciplined Paul. All that is claimed is that both Jesus and Paul were criminals before the law. One might ask here whether Jesus *was* a criminal before Jewish law, but that, if anything does, is beyond my brief.

24.81. If all men are criminals, it is likely that the criminal code of the Jews does not define criminals, as it emanates from them. It is a code that criminals have devised and is thus in *that* sense a 'criminal code'. So breaking the law may be one way of avoiding crime: 'But if I build up again those things which I tore down, then I prove myself a transgressor' (Gal.2:18).

24.82. To say that the Jewish legal system is in this sense a criminal code is to say something that Paul expressly denies, when he repudiates the question, whether 'the law is sin' with the asseveration 'By no means' (Rom.7:7).

24.83. Either we concede that Paul is, as ever on this topic, 'speaking with double tongue' (Moir *obiter dictum*) or we suggest that it is not the Jew of a Christian sort that here defends the law, but the Jew *tout court*. For the *Jew* the law is not against the law, man's law against God's; for the *Christian*, for *Paul* it is. Paul, the Christian Jew, here puts on the shoes of the non-Christian Jew.

24.84. At least, this legal system does not mirror the system in God's mind, but refracts it. From this law crime necessarily follows. Crime is not displayed by the breach of it, but is caused by obedience to it.

24.85. By gnawing at the corners of the law (eating ospreys is wrong <Lev.11:13>) Paul brings the whole edifice crashing down.

24.9. Paul found himself under no pressure to materialise the insights of his imagination: '... flesh and blood cannot inherit the kingdom of God' (1 Cor.15:50). Flesh and blood has 'flesh and bones' (Lk.24:39); what is not flesh and blood not. Luke's Paul is not Paul's Paul and generic analysis must analyse each differently. Luke is not so bad after all, provided that we rightly locate the logical status of his narrative propositions.

24.91. Paul's imagination is founded on broken hope: Jesus was dead and buried, but you cannot keep a good man down. Or a bad man either. Their 'heads', even when little that is admirable lies between their ears, must 'hammer through daisies' (13.87.). 'Unconsciously faith procures for herself all the illusions she needs for the conservation of her present possessions and for her advance to further conquests' (Loisy,1948, p.98). Broken hope can be a reliable foundation.

24.92. But not 'illusions'.

24.93. If we suppose that, when Paul says (1 Cor.15:50) 'Flesh and blood shall not inherit ...', he is attacking Luke's narrative style, that Luke's narrativity, or his *penchant* for telling stories, is under attack from Paul's narratology, his implicit (because he does not tell stories) critique of narrative theology, or that he is attacking narratives of the kind of which Luke's narrative is an example, then we may say that Paul, like Loisy, was not, in Gilbert Murray's phrase (Preface to Loisy, 1948, p.5), 'compelled to be uncritical'.

24.94. If Paul knows what is *not* the case, that post-mortem bodies will not be 'flesh and blood', does he know what *is* the case?

24.95. Paul was quite as capable of remaining silent on the lineaments of posthumous life as on the mental mechanics of crossing the threshold that led from Pharisaism to membership of a new group, even if he says enough to be 'at one with Judaism and the first generation of Christian writers in being indifferent to consistency in regard to matters as uncertain as the details of the life of the world to come' (Knox, 1939, p.141). One fine day he thought, like Peter (Loisy, 1948, p.130) he saw his master. That is enough. Jesus 'appeared' (1 Cor.15:8 <Greek: ophthe: 'he was seen'>), *scire licet* Paul saw the point of Christianity.

25.1. If one's case comes before the court, is it too much to hope that it will be the last case of its kind, that that will be the end of the matter? And what of the last case of *any* kind (2 Cor.5:10 'For we must all appear before the judgement seat of Christ ...)?

25.11. Is it too much to hope that the clerk of the court there will be 'writing with his pen in his cheek' (Boot, 1979, p.58)?

25.12. The logic of the language of '*last* judgement' is related to the language of 'judgement' as the figure 1 is related to the series: 1/2 2/3 3/4 4/5 ... 665/666 666/667 ... (Ramsey, 1960, p.121).

25.13. But why does it occur to Paul and to other Jews to use legal terms (e.g. *bema*, 'judgement seat' <2 Cor.5:10>)? Because Corinth has one, a *bema* that is (Scranton, 1951, pp.91 ff)?

25.15. Such a language is to be correlated with contemporary forensic practice, that is with forensic practice contemporary with Paul and with his discussants, those who saw logs with him in his forensic workshop.

25.16. But Paul inverts, stands on its head, stands on their heads, the 'early-prowling base-informing sad-litigious plaguy ways' (Aristophanes, *Wasps*, 505) of his contemporaries. Those against whom the case has clearly gone Paul's judge acquits.

25.17. We have to envisage a specially extended dock that can accommodate one hundred and forty four thousand (Rev.14:1 'Then I looked, and lo, ... a hundred and forty four thousand ...).

25.18. 'We must all appear ...' (2 Cor.5:10). It is important, Käsemann tells us (16.95.), that the case should be clearly lost. For it is not good that criminals should be allowed to remain innocent of their guilt.

25.19. 'We must all appear ... so that each one may receive good or evil, according to what he has done in the body', Paul goes on. Either Paul is saying *both* that 'a man is justified by faith' *and* that 'a man is justified by works', is acquitted in court on the basis of activity in conformity with law, *or* he is saying that the acquittal is of criminals who know that that is what they are: Paul's negative forensic observations function to clarify to the criminal what the case is, while they simultaneously foresee the judge's myopia, for the judge does not know a criminal when he cannot see one; Paul is retaining 'judgement' in order to destroy the criminal's illusions, but not to destroy the criminal.

25.2. The destruction of the criminals's illusions, rather than incoherence or inconsistency, is the best that can be said for Paul. It is another question whether it is justly said. Paul seems to expel 'judgement' with a fork; like nature, it seems to recur. It occurs to Paul to recur to this topic. *Should* he be doing so?

25.3. God is moving from 'I promise to do' to 'I do'.

25.31. What was promised was *Lebensraum*, children to fill the *Raum* and an active ally (Gen.17:4 ff 'Behold, my covenant is with you ... I will make you exceedingly fruitful ... I will give to you ... the land of your sojournings ...). (The Jews did not much suffer from unearthly conceptions).

25.32. What is *now* offered is insufflation: 'the promise of the spirit' (Gal.3:14).

25.33. This may be 'cashed', non-exhaustively, as a team of administrators and doctors. A more exhaustive list may be found at 1 Cor.12:28 'first apostles, second prophets ...'.

25.4. Paul's mind has a dramatic structure. He is author of a tragi-comedy. 'Plot', 'dénouement', *'deus ex machina'* belong to the interpreter's panoply (Dodd, 1920, pp.13 ff). (And not only Paul, but John is a dramatic writer: Pilate sends his 'posse' <Dodd, 1963, p.74; *ab esse ad posse valet consequentia* ?>.) And drama is more philosophical than history. But it is *not* history.

25.41. Paul's dramatic imagination, Paul the dramatist, emancipates his audience from history. He 'frees them from the past and opens them to the future' (Bultmann *passim*).

25.42. Bultmann and Paul may take us out of history, but they put us back into it again. Paul does 'circuits *and* bumps', he touches down again and again on 'the firm ground of history' (Käsemann *passim*).

25.43. But it is in the air that he shows his metal, well beyond 'the flaming ramparts of the world', high enough for the sky to gain the 'craftbound' name of 'heaven'.

25.44. There is an anlogy between speaking of Paul's dramatic imagination (Dodd) and of his 'symbolic universe' (Geertz, 1968).

25.5. By portraying God as an arbitrary and 'non-moral despot' (21.66.) Paul suggests to us that the way we order God's mind differs from the way God orders it himself.

25.51. Paul speaks of 'vessels of wrath made for destruction' (Rom. 9:22), 'to display both his (God's) absolute power and his entirely unmerited mercy on those whom he chooses to glorify' (O'Neill, 1975, p.159). There are places where Paul shows greater knowledge of pottery than he does of theology.

25.52. Men like pots are fragile ('... we have this treasure in earthen vessels ...' (2 Cor.4:7), but there is a difference between throwing a pot and dashing a man (or laywoman) to pieces. The right analogy for God is not the Herulian Goths, loose in the city of Corinth, but the archaeologist who re-assembles shards, cribbed in the museum workroom.

25.53. It is true that there were those 'Jews, who killed both the

Lord Jesus and the prophets and drove us out' (1 Thess.2:14 ff),
but the murder of judicial murderers is out of court here.

25.54. Or we can go with O'Neill to Endor and call up a glossator or
go to van Manen, for whom, if Paul wrote anything, we do not
have it.

25.6. Paul has an idealising imagination.

25.61. His imagination, idealising as it is, nevertheless does not lose
contact with the world as it is.

25.62. 'Crucifixion' is one among other terms that symbolises Paul's
hold on the real world and 'resurrection' his hold on , or, as he
himself might put it, his *being held by*, another world that runs
parallel to this one in such a way that it intersects with it at
every point. It is rather a single line that has breadth as well
as length. Or to use Ramsey's series (1960, p.121), in every
fraction the figure 1 is suggested or is implicit or is 'ingre-
dient' (Whitehead, 1979 *passim*). Or to use a Tillichian term
(1961, cit. Ross, 1981, p.145, fn.2), each fraction 'participates'
in the figure 1.

25.63. Paul's hold on the real world can be, if hesitantly, *inferred*
from his literary *topoi*. Whether his athletic expertise, for example, is due to wide reading or to hearsay or to athletic
outings on the Isthmus, it remains knowledge of a kind. Paul's
hold is *demonstrated* by his observations on the internecine
quarrels of the fissiparous Corinthians or on his ship that remained steady, because it was resting on the bottom of the
sea. His hold on the negative features of the real world is well
summed up in the gynaecological metaphor of Rom.8:22, where
he says that 'the whole creation has been groaning in travail
together until now'. His oriental pessimism does not permit
him to give vent to a comparable assessment of such positive
features as there really are. His work after all is anterior to
Teilhard de Chardin's *Phenomenon of Man* (1959) and Bonhoeffer's *Letters and Papers from Prison* (1959); two documents
that, unfashionably for Christians, *validate* the earth. Paul like
Buddhism, is always in danger of being too religious by half.

25.64. The *blik*, or viewpoint, at which Paul's idealising imagination
arrives is reached by *thinking away*, thinking away the negative features of the real world. The ideal rabbit then springs
full-grown from his hat.

25.7. Paul's correspondence on fund-raising and meat-marketing and
the like is sifficiently complex for his commentators to disagree on what is fundamental to it. But it would be agreed
that among those things that are fundamental to what he is

saying is not only the 'real absence' (23.5.) of Jesus, but his 'real presence': 'It is no longer I who live, but Christ who lives in me'. The word 'real' here, of course, is a historical assertion *only* in the sense that a historical agent, Paul, is making it, an assertion of the truth of which he is convinced, an assertion about a now *non-historical* agent.

25.71. Because Paul makes this assertion and is convinced that he can make it truly, his activity is doubtless other than it would otherwise be. If Jesus' death is no let to Jesus, nor Paul's to Paul, he feels he can speak his mind without fear or favour, even if some of his contemporary critics such as 'certain men ... from James' (Gal.2:12) found themselves free to deny that he always did so. For Paul's question, 'Am I trying to please men?' (Gal.1:10), implies that there were those that accused him of trying to do so. But, on the contrary, he is very 'bold', he 'says everything' (Greek: *parrhesia*: 2 Cor.3:12).

25.8. Maier, by his title (1977), whatever be his reasons for so entitling it, proclaims *The End of the Historical Critical Method*. *Tempus erat*, it is high time (the imperfect tense of the Latin verb is of a fact just realised).

25.81. Doubtless there remain stones to be exhumed, bones to be joined to his bone, and, the textual analogues of the archaeological enterprise, new questions to be put to old texts: '...the questions which are central for the classical scholar today are for the most part materially different, and nearly always differently form lated, from those on which attention was focused a hundred or even fifty years ago ... (I)n classical scholarship, as in all the historical sciences, the more usual and more important type of progress consists in the statement and solution of problems which are themselves entirely or partly new ... (I)t can also happen ... through a change in the focus of the scholar's eye' (Dodds, 1973, pp.27 ff). And some new texts may turn up to get 'put to the torture' in old ways and new. But the fact is that, if it is historical evidence that the historian needs, such evidence is provided sparely by Paul.

25.82. The *desideratum* is not a historical critical, but, if there is or can be such a thing, a theological critical method.

25.9. What Paul primarily provides, what, that is, he provides that is of primary importance, is 'G-statements' (Ross, 1969, pp. 164 ff), statements about God.

25.91. But it is arguable that 'G-statements' can only be or can also properly be (let those who know decide) approached through 'E-statements': 'statements about objects of natural experience' (Ross, *ibid.*).

25.92. And statements about human experience are just what the historian examines. And indeed even from Paul's G-statements some history may be inferred: from the statement, for example, that 'God ... leads us in triumph' (2 Cor.2:14), we may infer the feet of David's soldiery or of Alexander or of the Mummius, who sacked Corinth (146 B.C.), who had 'divine power to destroy strongholds' (2 Cor.10:4, Pauly-Wissowa, art. 'Mummius'), much as Paul had it, he thought, to 'destroy arguments' (2 Cor.10:5).

25.93. But if the historian studies human experience, such study does not belong to the historian alone.

25.94. For Freyne (obiter dictum) has honed his bugle for the announcement of a paradigm-shift from historical to literary enquiries. Freyne's war-cry was no 'indistinct sound; who will <not> get ready for battle?' (1 Cor.14:8 <with 'not' added>).

25.95. But, to ⸺ more, if no less, than to recall Aristotle's distinction (Poetics, 1451a), there is a difference in the human experience studied: the historian studies *actual*, the literary critic *possible* human experience, though thought, of course, can and perhaps must reconvert into possibilities the actualities of history.

25.96. But neither do history and literary criticism together exhaust the human sciences. Sociological studies are well under way, psychology, if not killed, has scotched the snake (Theissen, 1983 a). Anthropology, not in the sense of what theologians say man is, but of what social anthropologists say man is, is a largely untapped field. And philosophy, apart from Baur and Bultmann?

25.97. ''Tis not too late to seek a newer world' (Tennyson, *Ulysses*). 'Only if we abandon, in a phrase of Leo Steinbergs's (1953), that sweet sense of accomplishment which comes from parading habitual skills and address ourselves to problems sufficiently unclarified as to make discovery possible, can we hope to achieve work which will not just re-incarnate that of the great men of the first quarter of the century, but match it' (Geertz, 1968, p.2). But, Geertz adds: 'The dangers of such a procedure are obvious: arbitrary eclecticism, superficial theory-mongering, and sheer intellectual confusion. But I, at least, can see no other road of escape from what, referring to anthropology more generally, Janowitz (1963) has called the dead hand of competence'.

25.98. Have you no competence, you that pass by?

25.99. These remarks remain rant, a velleity, so long as the obligation they imply is not discharged.

26.1. Nor should it be forgotten that the theologian has to be able to 'exist in his own thinking' (the phrase is Kierkegaard's). Otherwise he may be doing something, but not theology. Nor should it be forgotten that he has to be prepared to cease to exist in his own thinking: *vivendo ac moriendo fit theologus* (Luther: 'a man becomes a theologian by living *and dying*).

26.2. Paul is not writing monographs that he has licked into shape like a whelp. His writing is fragmentary, *à tâtons*, 'groping'. Else how could Paul answer the question in Romans 3, 'What advantage has the Jew?' with 'Much in every way', in v.1 and with 'No, not at all', at v.9?

26.21. Or take into account the fact that Paul's narrative in 2 Cor. 2:12 f about Titus

26.22.

26.23. is only resumed in 2 Cor.7:5.

26.24. 'He is struggling to express what is in process of revelation to him' (Jowett, 1855, Vol.1, p.291). Is it possible to study not what Paul wrote, but how he came to write it? To re-enact in the theologian's own mind what went on in Paul's? How do we arrive not at what is there, but at how it *came to be* there?

26.3. Jesus of Nazareth once lived on the earth; now 'in the air', where we shall 'meet' him (1 Thess.4:17).

26.31. *Then* Jesus had no fixed abode. *Now* it is fixed in the sky. He has exchanged a 'tent' for a 'house' (2 Cor.5:1).

26.32. If 'Nazareth' is a guess and 'Nazarene' (Mt.2:23) tells us not that Jesus was from Nazareth, but that he was a 'man under vow' (Loisy, 1948, pp.69 f) and if we may infer from other evidence and from 'Foxes have holes ...; but the Son of man has nowhere to lay his head' (Mt.8:20; Lk.8:58), that Jesus, while he lived on earth, had no fixed abode (for 'the Son of man' means 'one does' and 'one does' means 'I do'), his abode is now fixed in the sky like a star, like a star that is brighter than other stars, 'for star differs from star in glory' (1 Cor.15:41).

26.33. And why does God live in the sky? And Jesus? And other men? And hypostatised, reified, personified information (7.1.)?

26.34. Whether in point of fact the spatial sense of 'up' is diachronically prior, or whether for the purpose of synchronic analysis it is merely convenient to take that usage first, there are other uses of 'up' that may be symbolised by the spatial sense.

26.35. One may be *superior* to one's enemy, even where one does not have one's foot on her neck. Tam was 'o'er a' the ills o' life victorious' (Burns, *Tam o' Shanter*).

26.36. 'Up' is an 'orientational metaphor' that 'organises a whole system of concepts with respect to one another' (Lakoff and

Johnson, 1980, p.14): 'Lazarus *rose* from the dead', 'my income *rose* last year' (*ibid.*, pp.15 f), 'God is *on top of* the situation', 'the faithful departed (the *high* spirits) are in *high* spirits'. And so on.

26.37. The metaphor 'licenses' (Ramsey's word *passim*) a plurality of analogous statements. Without being exhaustive, elements of that plurality are health, consciousness, happiness, power and status (Lakoff and Johnson, 1980, pp.15 ff).

26.38. In general it is true or at least seems to be implied that 'moral and spiritual worth is greater or less in ratio to the distance outwards from the earth's surface' (Bevan, 1962, p.26).

26.39. If it is also true that 'the number of books printed each year keeps going *up*' (Lakoff and Johnson, 1980, p.15), is this too an index of the moral and spiritual worth of the authors, by which the life of the readers is enhanced?

26.4. That God has on his shoulders a god*head* is plain.

26.41. It is a head around which one's head cannot be got.

26.42. But there is a partial knowledge, which may be represented by the interface between an observer and what he sees in a mirror: 'we see in a mirror dimly' (1 Cor.13:12 *'in einem dunklen Worte'*, 'in a dark word' <Brahms, *Vier Ernste Gesänge*>).

26.43. Paul's partial knowledge permits him, nevertheless, to haruspicate God's purposes. God's purpose in making laws, for example, is 'that every mouth may be stopped, and the whole world may be held accountable to God' (Rom.3:19). Law, evidently, only reveals a problem that law cannot solve. Law does not change society, but only makes necessary the extension of the prison system.

26.44. But 'the Semitic mind was notoriously unwilling to draw a sharp dividing-line between purpose and consequence' (Moule, 1959, p.142). As a good Semite, Paul is supposing that if the government of the cosmos is theocratic and if there is within that cosmos an effect E that follows from a cause C, it was certain that E would follow and it was known by God (and by Paul) to be certain to follow. Paul's 'identikit' of the godhead here can be perhaps enlarged so as to make plain that what Paul *really* means is that C occurred and E followed, but that theocracy is compromised by neither; the government does not fall: God made laws; men broke those laws; with *this* situation also God can cope.

26.5. Paul's religious language is built on certain root metaphors. Two of these metaphors are fundamental trust and the acquittal of the guilty. The first depicts the transcendent x-factor as a trustworthy friend; the second as an incompetent judge.

26.51. These metaphors are anecdotes without the narrative, parables *in nuce*, stories without narration.

26.52. Paul's religious language is 'originating' (Tracy, 1979). Paul's speech acts are among the first to follow the life of Jesus and have proved influential.

26.53. (But they should not be taken to inhibit other attempts, attempts to speak otherwise than Paul. The attempt to interpret Paul's interpretation of God does not demand that we do not attempt to interpret God. Speaking about Paul's theology does not bring about the closure of theology. <The remark is parenthetic.>)

26.54. Metaphors 'redescribe' (4.7.) reality and have cognitive force. What Judaism describes as judicial, Paul 'redescribes' as familial; God is father, not judge. Paul also uses judicial metaphors to make the familial point, but it is a familial point he is making.

26.55. That contrast between Judaism and Paulinism is, I suppose, just sufficiently crude to be unfair. Undeniably the systems overlap. Judaism is not without its familial, even *marital* features ('I will betroth you to me for ever' <Hosea 2:19>). But, even if it remains unclear whether Paul is relegating or is eliminating law, is it not also undeniable that the part played by law in Paul is no longer as for Judaism pre-eminent?

26.56. Paul's interpretations, if such a succinct writer can be called an interpreter, have chronological priority over most interpretations; they do not have logical or theological priority. Paul may criticise us, but we may criticise him. Homer nods. Paul was not always 'sleepless' (2 Cor.11:27).

26.6. The puzzling feature of theology is God.

26.61. The relation between God and Jesus of Nazareth or Jesus the Nazorean (26.32.) is, Paul holds, an iconic relation: for Jesus is 'the *likeness* of God' (*eikon*, 'icon': 2 Cor.4:4).

26.62. There are features of Jesus that are isomorphic with features of God. If light can be thrown on Jesus, light can be thrown on God.

26.63. To what extent does Paul's assertion of an iconic relation between Jesus and God remain a *mere* assertion? For Paul himself makes nothing of Jesus' easy commerce with the collaborating taxation officers of Herod Antipas and Rome and its analogue, the at least *finally* uncritical attitude of the judge, God, to the criminals brought before him. It takes Dodd (1932, p.58), not Paul, to draw the parallel in writing, which Dodd's Paul had drawn either silently or in speech that has not survived.

26.64. The statement that Jesus is like God is symmetric. From it follows the statement that God is like Jesus. So if Paul makes a statement about God, that statement also throws light on Jesus. From the forensic model, God is a judge who acquits the criminal, we can infer the historical statement that Jesus chose collaborating tax-farmers as his dinner companions; though we could not do so, if we did not have the Gospel narratives. *Tacet Paulus*, 'Paul is silent'.

26.65. Jesus is a clue to a field that is only partially known, the map of an imperfectly explored region.

26.7. One of the ways of doing theology is to say that, once you have said what you have said, there is more that you are not going on or cannot go on to say. There is, so to speak, a kind of 'logic of superabundance' in Paul: 'where sin increased, grace *abounded* all the more' (Rom.3:20), 'in all these things we are *more than* conquerors' (Rom.8:37).

26.71. And cognate with these comparatives is Paul's use of the word 'all' or 'every': 'that God may be everything to every one' (1 Cor.15:28). We do not win *some battles*, but *all wars*.

26.8. Jesus is the 'likeness' or 'icon' of God (2 Cor.4:4); is a 'parable' of God (Keck, 1972); is a model of God.

26.81. A model is to be distinguished from what it models.

26.82. Jesus is a scale-model of God: Jesus' working hands give some idea of the hands of God; is an 'analogue-model' (Black, 1962, p.222), whose behaviour shows structural affinity with the behaviour of God, his 'not pleasing himself', for example; is a 'heuristic fiction' (Mudge in Ricoeur, 1981, p.26), a root metaphor for God, who alerts us to relevant features of and provides categories for grasping God.

26.83. For if A is like B, then, in that we know A, we know as much of B as B is like A. In this sense, A sheds light on B; is a 'disclosure-model' (Ramsey, 1964, pp.9 f; and *passim*).

26.84. The relation between Jesus and God is a symbolic relation:
'1. There is an intimation that God is Jesus-like.
2. Jesus is taken as a condensed programme for exploration of God.
3. In carrying out this programme, expectations from Jesus are transposed to God as projective models.
4. For each of these projective models, aspects of God are seen to be related in Jesus-like ways, where we had not been attentive to those relations before.'
(Schon, 1963, p.64; 'God' has been substituted for Schon's 'B' and 'Jesus' for 'A'.)

26.9. 'Didst thou not pour me out like milk and curdle me like cheese?' Job 10:10 makes the connection between sexual reproduction, dairy-making and the activity of God (Ramsey, 1974, p.121; Gordis, 1978, pp.522 f; I thank Prof. Gibson for his help here <cf 6.43.>).

26.91. 'Only connect', says Margaret in *Howard's End*. 'Now I connect!' cries Agaue (Euripides, *Bacchae*, 1296). 'By far the greatest thing is the use of metaphor. That alone cannot be learnt; it is the token of genius. For the right use of metaphor means an eye for resemblances' (Aristotle, *Poetics*, 1459a; Dr. Mackenzie brought this quotation to my notice), sc. the power of detecting identity in difference.

26.92. Paul connects the activity of Jesus with the repatriation of prisoners or the manumission of slaves and both with the activity of God: there is 'redemption ... in Christ Jesus' (Rom. 3:24).

26.93. Paul makes *connections, synopses.*

27.1. 'Creation' differs from 'world' as 'God's world' differs from 'the world' *tout court*. There is the world and there is the Gworld (read: God's world).

27.11. And there is Jerusalem and GJerusalem (read: God's Jerusalem).

27.12. GJerusalem is 'above' (Gal.4:26), *up* not *down.* 'Above' is Paul's 'qualifier' (Ramsey, 1967). The way to the metaphorical city is signposted by the 'orientational metaphor' (26.36.). The city is reached by prescinding from thought-police, the enforcement of bye-laws and from the drainage canals, 'from 1.78 to 2.36m. (5 ft. 10 ins. to 7 ft. 9 ins.) high and from 0.76 to 0.91 m. (28 to 36 ins.) broad', of the Jerusalem that is below (Jeremias, 1969, p.17). The Christian has blessed assurance of better drainage. And GJerusalem differs from Jerusalem in being twice more than 'half as old as time', the Jerusalem that God 'showed ... to Adam before he sinned' (2 Bar.4:3).

27.13. Paul replaces a city by a city, a commonwealth with a commonwealth (Phil.3:20 'our commonwealth is in heaven'). To conjoin images from the same lexical field, which Paul does not conjoin, Paul is an 'ambassador' (2 Cor.5:20) to the colonies.

27.14. And 'heaven' differs from 'sky' as Gsky differs from sky.

27.15. If the word 'sky' has lost its symbolic force, does the word 'heaven' retain it?

27.16. Substituting city for city, commonwealth for commonwealth, is tantamount to setting up an alternative state; or an alternative state to the state, which is reached by prescinding from, *thinking away* the negative features of the empirical state.

27.17. But the empirical state, the harlot astride the beast, Messalina, is impatient of alternatives. In so far as Paul envisages an alternative, Paul *ist ein politischer Mensch* (Käsemann, *obiter dictum*), 'is a political animal'. If it is true that there is an alternative state, it is a truth that endangers states and *die Wahrheit ist immer staatsgefährdend*, 'truth always endangers states' (anon., porter in Karlsruhe).

27.18. Paul is thinking of God's body politic. It differs from 'the unhesitating physicality of John's symbol for heavenly things' (Farrer, 1964, p.4 <Rev.>) in being more urbane.

27.19. Paul's mind has been persuaded to seek for an alternative: first to posit one, then to affirm what has been posited: *let there be* another Jerusalem; there *is* another Jerusalem. What has been posited and then affirmed retains a connection with the question it was intend to answer: what is wrong with this Jerusalem? Is there another Jerusalem? If the question takes a 'Jerusalem' form, the answer will take a 'Jerusalem' form.

27.2. Jesus 'appeared to Cephas' (1 Cor.15:5). Loisy speaks of Peter's 'fugitive visions, almost dreams, perhaps dreams' (*'de légères visions, presque des songes, peut-être des songes'*: 1933, p.131, my tran.).

27.21. Whether Paul had a dream or imagined vigorously or whether 'the ice broke, the penny dropped or the light dawned' for him (Ramsey, 1967, *passim*); whether by deduction or inference he 'saw the point', can only be conjectured, for we cannot unpack a case that has been left at Troas.

27.3. Being shorter than Proust or Plato, Paul never offers a full analysis, never holds, as *Hamlet*, 'as 'twere a mirror up to nature' (for the phrase: *Hamlet*, III, ii, 24). With a triumphant air, with self-satisfied prestidigitation, Paul produces out of his hat a single term.

27.31. Such as 'boasting'.

27.32. In his classical article, Jonas shows what can be done with it (1971, pp.333 ff). The predicament signified by 'boasting', translated into lapidary Latin, resides in a rotating or oscillatory movement around or between *velle me velle* and *cogitare me velle*; there is, that is, a movement around or between a conscious involvement with persons, objects or situations, which in Jonas' view, cannot but terminate in a self-conscious involvement with *oneself*, until a change of mind reverses the pendulum or sets the wheel in motion again; there is a necessary transition from being an actor to being a spectator; or, in

other words, there is a transition from the cor excurvatum ex
se to the cor incurvatum in se, from 'the heart turned outwards' to 'the heart incurved upon itself'. In Jonas' view (and
Jonas' view is that his view is or is implied by Paul's) a man
cannot rescue himself from this predicament, his bootstraps
must be pulled by another: of the possibility, that 'this, of itself endless dialectic (can) be halted from somewhere else
philosophy has nothing to say' (op. cit., p.341).

27.33. But there are philosophers who would deny this self-denying
ordinance. Whitehead's God 'lures' (1979) or Whitehead is no
philosopher. Theology is a special area of philosophy.

27.4.   Paul had his critics.

27.41. What Paul's critics asserted has to be inferred from what Paul
denied.

27.42. Paul's mien was sufficiently corrugated for there to stick to
him some of the mud thrown at him: it is likely that his critics had a case to make and Paul a case to answer. The case
for 'circumcision' as a liminal procedure is not much weaker
than the case for 'baptism'.

27.43. And the case Paul makes against the one ('circumcision') is not
much less strong than the case he did not make, but might
have made against the other ('baptism'). 'If we take Paul's
argument to its logical conclusion ... (i)t may well be doubted
whether in the last resort Paul would not have equated baptism with circumcision, as being a significant rite but not essential to salvation' (Neil, 1967, p.90).

27.44. 'We have to reckon, if we are honest, with a strongly antinomian element in Christianity as a historical phenomenon. It
shows itself in the New Testament in Paul's bitter arguments
with himself concerning the Jewish law ...' (Mackinnon, 1963,
p.16 <14.86.>). It is certain that this 'antinomian element' did
not win the support of those for whom legality is tidy.

27.45. So Paul had to provide his own support, blow his own trumpet
('I worked harder than any of them' 1 Cor.15:10) and write his
own references or claim that Jesus had written them for him,
for posthumous publication and apostolic post: 'you show that
you are a letter from Christ delivered by us' (2 Cor.3:3).

27.46. The tetchiness of this text, called 'coruscating' (18.53.), is only
equalled by its complexity: 'The sharp shifts of metaphor make
it extremely difficult to fit all the elements of this passage
into a coherent pattern ...' (Murphy-O'Connor, 1983, p.170).

27.47. Lambrecht (1983, p.367, fn. 56) has excavated some further
mild objurgations: Paul's transition is 'quaintly syncopated'
(Moule, 1972); Paul 'is clearly in a mess' (Hooker, 1980-81,
p.296); 'without his noticing the picture has changed' (Her-

mann, 1961, p.27: *'Unversehens hat sich das Bild verwan-
delt ...'*). But whatever the obscurities of the passage, it is not
unfair to say that Paul's defence of his apostolic office is, in
part at least, a defence of his post office (18.53.).

27.5.   The Christian religion is supposed to be a religion of love
(Henderson, *obiter dictum*).

27.51. Despite appearances to the contrary, the Christian religion *is* a
religion of love.

27.52. 'Love', the root metaphor of Christianity (Tracy, 1979) is a
category out of which Paul does not get much mileage. And
this, despite the song Paul sings (1 Cor.13).

27.53. In Gal.2:19 ff, where Paul speaks of being 'crucified with
Christ' and of 'the Son of God, who loved me and gave himself
for me', a single participle of the verb, 'to love', covers at
least the time from Jesus' birth to his death, if the 'death',
implied on the one hand by *Paul*'s crucifixion and the preposition, 'with', that goes with it, and on the other by 'gave
himself for me', is synecdoche for the beginning and middle
which led to the end.

27.54. Bultmann speaks *passim* of the 'mere that', the 'mere fact
that Jesus once existed'. Here in Gal.2:20 is Paul's 'mere
how': he 'loved me'. Brevity is the soul of Paul's wit.

27.55. The theologian is under obligation to take language to its limit. In its theological use, 'love' transcends, while it includes,
the ties of consanguinity and passion.

27.6.   The theological correlate of 'one is known' (1 Cor.8:3) is 'one
does not know' or 'one knows in part' (1 Cor.13:12); of 'I have
gone to sleep' 'I will be wakened'; of 'I am enabled' 'I cannot',
for 'our competence is from God, who has made us competent'
(2 Cor.3:5).

27.61. There are some active verbs of which men cannot be the subjects: e.g. 'I know', 'I undertake to live when I am dead', 'I
can'.

27.7.   Theologians have data, such as 'Jesus has been wakened'.

27.71. Theological data have, of course, to be distinguished from historical data, such as 'the bones of Jesus lie somewhere in the
State of Israel' (5.5.).

27.72. More importantly, the theologian has, or thinks he has, a *dans*
and a *daturus*, a giver and one who will give. We are dealing
not only with a 'deposit'; we are obliged not only to 'guard
what has been entrusted' (1 Tim.6:20) to us, but to hold open a
ready sack. The opponents of the Montanists do not have it all
their own way. The Montanists have it all their own way.

27.73. A tradesman who has a hire-purchase agreement is likely to be as little satisfied with one instalment as a farmer with one sack of grain when there are still ears in the wind.

27.8. Jesus of Nazareth never wrote a book in his life. That he once wrote on sand (Jn.8:6) is not reliable.

27.81. It is possible or probable that Paul is the earliest writer of the Jesus school that we have. The system of images he came up with has exercised an extraordinary, and in some ways mischievous, grip on subsequent imagination.

27.82. Paul's *Urworte*, Paul's 'primal words' , 'originating words' (the term is <somewhere> Buber's), are not final; and we cannot be content with ''cohobation' whereby from a single temporal substance diverse distillates are derived, which then ossify as the quaint world-views of discontinuous epochs' (Hart, 1968, p.41). Theology is on the way out, is nothing if not itinerant. And interpreting texts about God is no substitute for interpreting God. If God has a pen in his hand, he has not hung up his boots. If he has written texts, he has also written supplements to texts, that are themselves texts. God is not, so to speak, *emeritus*.

27.83. But if others have written, so has Paul. And Paul's texts demand interpretation. Or, if 'demand' is too strident, Paul's texts 'lure' (27.33.) the interpreter.

27.84. The action of God is the texts he inspires and of man the texts he hinders.

27.85. That is not to say that the activity of God is exhausted by his textuality. It is natural for scholars to over-rate texts, just as it is natural for churchmen to over-rate cult. But *if* elsewhere, then here *also*. The bait by which the interpreter is lured is sometimes edible. There are texts that reward close reading.

27.9. Paul claims that he is a 'minister of a new covenant' (2 Cor. 3:6).

27.91. The phrase is odd. You cannot 'serve an alliance'. You can keep the allies in line; you can co-opt new members; you can be an ally yourself and behave as one.

27.92. You can serve the allies, serve the 'covenanters'. You can 'be for' (23.35.) the Corinthians, for they are 'a letter from Christ delivered by us' (2 Cor.3:3), where 'delivered by us' can also mean, and perhaps should mean, 'served by us' or 'ministered to by us' (which would make Paul's 'apostolic office' not postal <27.47.>, but menial). And you can be for the Corinthians, but not only them, but also the Thessalonians and ...; indeed, for all men.

27.93. Perhaps Paul is a 'minister of a new covenant' in that the Gcovenanter (read: 'God') has, like the Crown, appointed Paul to be his minister.

28.1. The term 'covenant' is very wide. It can be used to unite two persons, two families, two clans, two nations, or more. Political animals make political agreements: compacts, treaties, contracts: agreements between citizens, groups of citizens, nations. Here is a political metaphor.

28.11. The agreement of which Paul is speaking here is to be distinguished from the agreement entered into by Moses and God. Or rather the Jews and God, Moses being the Jewish representative or chief negotiator. A code of practice is drawn up that specifies how the allies are to behave, a code more wordy, more sesquipedalian, for the Jews than for God. There is a dinner to celebrate the occasion, though the blood goes not, as it were, into the haggis, but half of it onto the diners and the other half onto the table: 'And Moses took half of the blood ... and half of the blood he threw against the altar ... and Moses took the blood and threw it upon the people ...' (Ex.24:6, 8). The allies become blood-brothers: 'I am yours and you are mine'.

28.12. Paul's agreement differs from the earlier version as an international from a national version. The code of practice is unspecified. The forging of the agreement is celebrated by regular dinners: 'Go, eat your bread with enjoyment, and drink your wine with a merry heart' (Eccl.9:7, cit. Bonhoeffer, 1983, pp.132 f, 'The Right to Bodily Life').

28.13. But wine is blood-red.

28.14. In the course of setting up the treaty, Jesus infringed God's space, created a nuisance within the precincts of God's house.

28.2. To say that 'the cleansing of the temple' caused Jesus' death is to supply from elsewhere what Paul does not himself supply. What Paul tells us is that Jesus lost his life in attempting to set up the treaty, or 'cut' (in the Hebrew idiom) the covenant.

28.21. Paul's perspective on the aims of Jesus is the perspective of that part of the movement that criticised Moses' code of practice.

28.22. The wing of the corporation to which Paul belonged did not take kindly to the application of purely Jewish rules to non-Jewish members. Foreskins were not to be waved, but waived.

28.23. In 2 Cor.3, Paul declares himself to be not primarily (or not at all?) interested in codifying human response to a non-human agent, but in clarifying the nature of the non-human agency to which men are responding.

28.3. How does Paul come to decide that 'covenant' is an appropriate image for describing the mutual relations of God and man? And what angularity in the Jesus story provides the hook for Paul to hang it on?

28.31. Paul is under the domination of linguistic practice. As one of the earlier of the early Christians, he is influenced by the speaking habits of Christians earlier than he. If Christianity is, which it is, merely a more adequate version (so Christians think) of Judaism, it is not surprising that Christians should be influenced by Jewish ways of speaking.

28.32. And those Jewish ways of speaking are anchored in the political arrangements to the West of the fertile crescent.

28.33. And those political arrangements of the Semites are themselves anchored in arrangements that antedate the evidence. 'For, in a sense, all human covenanting in its infinite variety is but the outcome and expansion of a primal covenant, whereby some little group of scarcely human folk, moved by some purblind sense or sentiment of association, exchanged unspoken vows to stand or fall together ... Some (sc. anthropologists) ... would exalt the authority of a Cyclopean sire, citing none too well authenticated parallels from the social habits of gorillas, with whom they are not likely to have been in personal contact. Others, with whom I would myself rather side, would allow to the united mothers, who would presumably be the more sedentary members of the primitive home, a certain control over their offspring, that might go a long way towards preventing domestic anarchy; more especially if the mere male was inclined to be cowed by a sex at once so mysterious and so vocal' (Marett, 1933, p.160).

28.34. The hook in Jesus' life on which the notion hangs is his death. Paul, as his Christian predecessors surely, 'connects' (26.91.) Jesus' blood shed with a covenant made, an alliance struck. Death, feasting, agreement all 'implode'. Men meet together and they dine; God meets with them and dines with them.

28.35. And the host at dinner, to use *that* metaphor, is, metaphorically speaking, himself the dinner, to use *that* one too.

28.4. There is a distinction between the relation a sergeant has with his platoon, and the relation Jesus has with the Christian, whom Jesus 'lures', from whom he invites a response. Jesus is (2 Cor.10:1) 'meek and gentle', is humane in his responses.

28.41. Paul speaks of 'the obedience of faith' (Rom.1:5). It is perhaps a hendiadys.

28.42. But what are the *two* of which *one* is made? For 'the way of near-absolute obedience is the way that helps make possible the Belsens, the Dachaus and the Auschwitz's of the twentieth century. There is indeed an element of paradox that the contribution to ethics by some at least of those thinkers most cocerned to be *avant-garde* should peter out in vacuous arguments on behalf of what is called radical obedience. No virtue is surely more deeply questionable than obedience' (Mackinnon, 1974, p.105).

28.43. Despite Barr's warning (1961) that etymology can be a bad guide to use, it may nevertheless in any instance be asked whether etymology and semantics do in fact diverge. And in any case warnings can be ignored.

28.44. The root of Paul's word in Rom.1:5 means to 'listen to', to 'hear'. And this 'all the gods' do in Homer (*Iliad* 8:4), but, mind you, it is Zeus that is talking and 'all the gods' that are listening and what they are listening to is the promise to hurl anyone who gets out of step into Tartarus which is 'as far beneath Hades as heaven is above the earth' (*ibid.* 13-16).

28.45. If *Iliad* 8:4 is of doubtful assistance, we may move from the Greek of Homer to the Greek of Athenaeus, the 2nd or 3rd cent. A.D. grammarian, who uses the word to speak of 'accepting an invitation to dinner' (247d).

28.46. But we do not need to be baulked by Homer and encouraged by Athenaeus to be persuaded that in dealing with language we are dealing with '*differentiation* (contrasting adaptation to context), *fit* to diversity of linguistic environment' (Ross, 1981, p.6).

28.47. What is the *Pauline* environment?

28.48. The immediate environment of 'obedience of faith' in Rom.1:8 is on the one hand that Paul is a 'slave' and Jesus his 'slave-master' and on the other that Paul is a 'son' and God his 'father', who loves the Romans in Rome and Paul as he writes at Corinth in the winter of 56/57 — and, Jewett (1979) would add, writing at ten to three on a January afternoon.

28.49. But 'slave' and 'slave-master' are ambiguous and may be weakened to 'one who is repectful' and 'the person he respects'. It may be added, too, that there may be subtle (and not so subtle) differences between the Jewish family of Paul's day, God's family as Paul pictured it, and our own. If the sociologist has much to say about the first and the last, how much more ought not to be said of the second? At any rate it is clear that the father of Edmund Gosse (1916) differs *toto cae-lo* from the father of McLeod Campbell, whose father 'in heaven' has some of the characteristics of his own, who 'by a shocking decree ... was ordered by his Presbytery to read from his pulpit a paper condemning his son's doctrines, and warning people against listening to his preaching. He refused' (Dickie in Campbell, 1959, p.xiv). For '(t)here had always been and there always endured, a wonderful relation between them' (ibid.).

28.5. Is Paul's *diction* striking?

28.51. There is a correlation between the secular experience of Paul and the language in which he expresses his experience. We have, of course, no access to his experience other than through the language he uses to express it. Paul often did not sleep at night. He tells us he had 'many a sleepless night'. Had we been there, we might have heard him tossing and turning. Or Phoebe's knock.

28.52. There is a correlation between the secular experience of Paul, expressed in language, and his religious experience, expressed in religious language. Jesus did fall asleep. He was wakened. He lives closely with Paul. Paul finds him fascinating. 'Sleeping', 'waking', 'living with' are 'unbound' terms that can find place in both secular and religious discourse.

28.53. How instructive would it be to turn the tables on conventional practice and use secular language in religious contexts and *vice versa*, to use extra-cultic language within the cult and *vice versa*, to use *profane* language *in* the fane, to turn the *altars* on conventional practice?

28.54. To what extent is Paul's diction *religious* diction? Living in Jerusalem has its problems. There is possibly another place. There is actually another place. Let us call it 'Jerusalem'.

28.55. The gap between what Paul is getting and what he wants takes a 'Jerusalem' shape. Here the police are 'negligent or brutal' (Renan, 1869, p.5). He wants a community of a different kind from the one he has, but he uses the same name for both towns, adding, however, *'up'*. Spice 'Jerusalem' with 'up' and what do you get? 'Jerusalem'.

28.6. But how striking is Paul's diction?

28.61. Bultmann (1910, p.91) does not say that when Paul went down town he kept his eyes shut, but he says something very like it: admitting first that Paul is shorter than Calvin, 'one cannot agree in this with Heinrici, that Paul 'clear-sightedly handed himself over to the impressions of the cities' (p.574). His comparisons, as far as we can survey them, demonstrate the opposite: for the colourful life about him he had no open eyes'. If Paul was not struck, it is unlikely he should be able to write strikingly.

28.62. Paul follows mostly 'the clichés of Greek rhetoric' (Meeks, 1983, p.9). When he says that 'the weapons of our warfare are

not worldly but have divine power to destroy strongholds'
(2 Cor.10:4), this does not mean that he has evinced an interest
in the torsion catapults with which Philip failed to take Perin-
thus in 340. It means that what was familiar to some of Paul's
predecessors and contemporaries was familiar to Paul by hearsay or 'readwrite'. Paul knew that a wise man wanting out of
a city should keep his basket about him (2 Cor.11:33), but he
knew no more about entering one by storm than he got from a
rapid reading of Prov.21:22: 'A wise man scales the city of the
mighty and brings down the stronghold in which they trust'.
(With the help of his God and the sweat of his comrades Paul
was not one to prefer leaping to being lowered).

28.63. Of course, you can write vividly about what you have not ex-
perienced yourself, but you have to diverge from the commonplace in order to qualify as a vivid writer.

28.64. But it was Wilamowitz-Möllendorf, who said that with the
writing of Paul a new vitality enters Greek prose: that 'at
last, at last someone is speaking again in Greek about an experience of life that comes from the heart and is fresh' ('... von
einer frischen inneren Lebenserfahrung' (1905, p.107).

28.65. Why did he say that?

28.7. 'Like a good Hellenistic moralist, Paul puts forth his own life
as a model to be imitated, but by his 'biography of reversal'
(Schütz, 1975, p.133) and his application of the Cross as a
metaphor to his own mishaps and sufferings, he transforms
that commonplace into something new' (Meeks, 1983, p.131).

28.71 In 2 Cor.4:10 Paul says that we are 'always carrying in the
body the death of Jesus'.

28.72. The verb 'carrying' suggests the dead weight of the crossbeam
and upright of a cross. The descent to Avernus is difficult.

28.73. This is a startling synizesis of Jesus' last journey and Paul's
quotidian experience. Life is a tumbril.

28.74. But the tumbril will be replaced by heavenly transport (for
death merely masks life), the tumbril by the chariot of fire.
As so often, so predictably, Paul's talk of death is comple-
mented by his talk of life. For he continues (2 Cor.4:10): '... so
that the life of Jesus may also be manifested in our bodies'.
And again (vv.13 f): 'we too believe ..., knowing that he who
raised the Lord Jesus will raise us also with Jesus and bring us
with you into his presence'.

28.75. Käsemann points out that life which is subsequent to death in
v.14 is simultaneous with it in v.10, provided that the final
clause in the latter can be construed as logical rather than
temporal: 'In a typically Pauline paradox (cf. 2 Cor.4:10-13) the
sequence of suffering and glorification with Christ (Rom.8:17c

'in order that we may also be glorified with him') is set in the mode of contemporaneity ... Grace ... thrusts the community and each of its members beneath the cross where extreme assault and victory coincide' (Käsemann, 1980, pp.231 f).

28.76. 'Crucifixion' and the life of Paul here 'interact' (Black, 1962, pp.25 ff). Paul's life is cruciform.

28.77. Bultmann (1976, p.118) denies that 'the dying of Jesus is a pictorial expression ('ein bildlicher Ausdruck') for the suffering that encounters the man who takes his (sc. Jesus') side' and asserts that 'the participation in Jesus' death is the real experience ('die reale Erfahrung') of the power of death that is at work in the death of Jesus' (my trans.).

28.78. But why oppose 'pictorial' and 'real'? Why not say, 'Real and pictorial'? Or 'real and metaphorical'? For '... an emphatic, indispensable metaphor does not belong to the realm of fiction, and is not merely being used, as some writers allege, for some mysterious aesthetic effect, but really does say something ...' (Black, 1979, p.41).

28.8. Is Paul telling the truth?

28.81. In such contexts as these Black is hesitant about the word 'truth' as 'the epithet 'true' has more restricted uses than philosophers usually recognise' (ibid., p.40). Black prefers to speak of 'correctness and incorrectness' and insists that 'this is the clue we need in order to do justice to the cognitive, informative, and ontologically illuminating aspects of strong metaphors', which 'can properly be held to convey, in indispensable fashion, insight into the systems to which they refer. In this way, they can, and sometimes do, generate insight about 'how things are' in reality' (ibid., p.41). If New Testament mythology is capable of communicating something about ontology to the reader of Heidegger's Being and Time, then metaphor also to the theorist or literary critic. For what is myth, if it is not, though not exhaustively, a constellation of 'strong' metaphors?

28.9 The images that explain the lives of Jesus, Paul, Paul's companions and correspondents are like the mailbags collected en route by an express train. The mailbags are picked up because they are there to be picked up and because there is a net on the train to pick them up. They have 'empirical fit' (4.97.).

28.91. That Paul had a hard time is the net that picks up 'the death of Jesus' in 2 Cor.4:10.

28.92. That Jesus was dying and that he died are historical facts. That Paul was dying and that he died is an image, unless when Paul wrote this he was writing posthumously.

28.93. The historical facts of Jesus' career provide Paul with imagery to explain his own career.

28.94. Much as the historical facts of the Israelite amphictyony, its political arrangements, its leagues, provided them with imagery for explaining their theological facts, their 'history' with Jehovah.

29.1. The word that means 'covenant' or league in 2 Cor.3:6 'differentiates' (Ross, 1981, *passim*) to mean 'will' in Gal.3:15 'no-one annuls even a man's will'.

29.11. Paul calls this 'a human example' (Gal.3:15).

29.12. Paul need not have told us this. He has been doing nothing else all along. 'Justification', 'redemption', 'atonement', 'spirit', what you will — these are all 'human examples'. There is no statement in theology that is not 'a human example'.

29.13. What Paul is giving us here is 'a human example' that is qualified as such, as opposed to giving us 'a human example' qualified as divine.

29.14. Either one gives 'human examples' and negates them, as when one speaks of God's 'apathy' (the privative 'a' negates his '-pathy', his passion) or one gives 'human examples' and out-trumps them: God is not wise, but wiser than wise. *Ramsey locutus*, Ramsey has told us (1967), *causa finita*, 'the case is closed'.

29.2. God is a member of the league and stands by it: it is an 'eternal' league.

29.21. In his testamentary dispositions God makes over to us his property, his real, or most real, estate, but it is not true that he has died. He has started the hand-over for tax purposes while still living. No codicil may be added without the client's authorisation. The red tape must remain tied, the seal unbroken.

29.3. What is the logic of Paul's epistolary propositions? They must not be misconstrued. It is to misconstrue them to read them other than as 'qualified models' (Ramsey, 1967), as 'heuristic fictions' (26.82.).

29.4. Paul got himself into so much hot water (and cold water, for the matter: his ship sank under him <2 Cor.11:25> three times) that he cannot have been one to keep his mouth buttoned.

29.41. Like the sex that is 'at once so mysterious and so vocal' (28. 33.) Paul said everything to everyone on every occasion: Paul had 'boldness' (2 Cor.3:12). When Paul saw (Horace's) 'black wind' (Odes I.V.7), he simply put on more sail. He published and was damned. But not by God. Or if by God, then not always by God. 'Though he slay me (and he does), yet will I trust in him' (Job 13:15 AV <RSV is less optimistic: 'Behold, he will slay me; I have no hope'>).

29.42. Paul made things difficult for himself, for not only was his travel agent irresponsible, but his opponents were 'ticklish in their absolute presuppositions' (Collingwood, 1940, p.31). They blew up in Paul's face. Paul relativised law, where his opponents absolutised it.

29.43. As well as 'bowels' (Phil.2:1 <AV>, 'affection' <RSV>) Paul had guts.

29.44. Democracies, it is said, enjoy freedom of speech; it is a characteristic of being a friend that one speak one's mind.

29.45. A Cynic would add, with William Blake, the courage to enjoy sexual congress in one's back garden.

29.46. By 'freedom of speech', 'boldness', Paul means 'openness' (Bultmann, 1976, p.88) or 'the courage to be open, to speak openly about something'. Fiat audacia, ruat coelum: 'I will be bold, though the sky fall'. Without recking the consequences, Paul puts forward his internationalist views to a nationalist audience, puts Moses in the shade: 'what once had splendour has come to have no splendour at all ...' (2 Cor.3:10).

29.5. Paul was a political animal (27.17.).

29.51. Politically he was a Roman citzen, theopolitically a citizen of Jerusalem, sc. the new town, Jerusalem.

29.52. Geographically his origin was Tarsus, 'uranographically' Jerusalem. Paul had a dual citizenship.

29.53. At the level of secular politics, of geopolitics, Paul is not defending Jews against anti-semitism, but Gentiles against 'anti-gentilism' or non-Jews against anti-non-Judaism.

29.54. God is a political animal.

29.55. As a religious citizen of the new Jerusalem, as one of God's citizens from God's city, Paul is merely adopting God's political views: God is against being against non-Jews. God insists that justice be done to non-Jews also and be seen to be done, even if 'seen' has to be understood in its Pickwickian sense: justice has to be 'unseen' to be done.

29.6. Cult is one of the luxuries of the church-going classes.

29.61. So it might be said.

29.62. Yes, but it might also be said that cult is one of the necessities of the human animal as such.

29.63. Cult or ritual is a sequence of activities which are intended to shed light on all activities.

29.64. Cult consists of a congeries of heuristic fictions.

29.65. Cult activities are very commonly carried out in a dwelling house or in a building like a dwelling house; in God's house, that is, or in a house where God is the owner-occupier with large 'policies' (O.E.D. 'policy', sb^1, II c: '... demesne land').

29.66. The resident in *this* house is worth all that the mayor is worth (15.6.) 'and more' (Ramsey, *passim*). Here is a very real resident, a very real house, an *ens realissimum* in a *domus realissima*.

29.7. By listening to the heuristic fictions that are spoken in *this* house and by being a spectator of the heuristic *actions* that are enacted here, a man can acquire a perspective on all thought and action, a perspective, for example, that makes death not terminal, that reminds us, when things are difficult, that we are not closeted with nullity as a widow with her bed: '... even though I am nothing' (2 Cor.12:11), I am a 'new creation' (2 Cor.5:17 <6.17.>).

29.71. In *this* house God is given his *worth*. A certain valuation is set here on his services.

29.72. But we do not need *this* house to do *that* in, for there is 'Worship in Everyday Life', to quote the title of Käsemann's essay (1969). An argument in Antioch can be the place where or the occasion on which Paul shows Peter what value he, Paul, accords to God's political opinions. Or, if that was an argument that interrupted a service in God's house, still it can hardly be maintained that the 'spiritual worship' (Rom.12:1 <'reasonable service' AV>) is to be located only in a house theologically qualified as God's: 'there is in principle an abandonment of the cultic sacred place which is characteristically a place of divine worship for the ancient world ... Sacred times and sacred places are superseded by the eschatological public activity of those who at all times and in all places stand 'before the face of Christ' and from this position before God make the everyday round of so-called secular life into the arena of the unlimited and unceasing glorification of the divine will' (Käsemann, 1969, p.191). Käsemann (p.192, fn.10) aptly recalls Rom.14:14: 'I know and I am persuaded in the Lord Jesus that nothing is unclean in itself; but it is unclean for any one who thinks it unclean' and comments (1980, p.375): 'it removes for Christians the basic distinction of all antiquity, which is still influential today, between the cultic sphere and the profane'.

29.8. Paul was a proponent of secular Christianity.

29.81. If Käsemann is right (and in a discipline such as theology in which 'there is no view that is not held by someone' <*'in der*

Theologie gibt es nichts was es nicht gibt', Käsemann, *obiter dictum*>, and good money is spent to acquire it, and where correctness anywhere above the level of the lower criticism <aptly so called> can only be a matter of fighting certainty, why should he not be right?), it remains remarkable the extent to which discourse drawn from old Judaea's holy fane has infected Paul's pen: Paul's imagination is, if more abstractly, parasitic on his Hebrew forebears.

29.82. Among the language-games Paul plays is a game with the Isthmian games (or with the literary analogues of Graeco-Roman athletics generally). But among them also is the cultic game; sometimes the cultic game for cultic purposes, sometimes for secular purposes.

29.83. The bread and wine of 1 Cor.11 are components of a cultic meal. The meal, it is true, is profane in the technical sense, as eaten outside the temple area of God's house, and what is eaten and drunk is profane in so far as bread and wine belong equally well to 'unbound' as to 'craftbound' actions. Nevertheless cult is implied by 'the mystical relation of bread and wine to the commemoration of (Jesus') saving death, of which the Supper is, in a manner, the mystical reiteration' (Loisy, 1948, p.82).

29.84. Whereas Käsemann speaks, somewhere, of 'the profane language of the parables', it should be noted also that Paul uses cultic language for profane purposes: God put Jesus forward 'as an expiation by his blood' (Rom.3:25); an execution outside the walls of the city of Jerusalem is modelled in language that has been exhumed inside the walls of God's house within the city.

29.85. A simpler example: The Corinthians such as they were, a profane lot, one imagines, are, corporately or severally, 'a temple of the Holy Spirit' (1 Cor.6:19).

29.86. And if lexemes from the lexical field of the cult can shed light on the profane, there is no reason why not, conversely, a profane vocabulary, whether of Jesus, Paul or ourselves, should shed light on the sometimes Cimmerian obscurities of the cult. Let the Sciopods but shift their feet and the 'light will dawn' (Ramsey, *passim*).

29.9. Paul was too busy writing the New Testament to be capable of quoting from it.

29.91. Paul does not have his pennies, his *denarii*, from an earthen pot. His 'treasure', like a hoard of gold coins of Philip and Alexander (Edwards and Thompson, 1970 <I thank Mr. Orestes Zervos for this reference>), is '*in* earthen vessels' (2 Cor.4:7) but does not originate there. His *denarii*, his *staters* rather, are dropping from heaven.

29.92. 'Dropping from the veils of the morning to where the cricket sings' (W.B.Yeats).

29.93. The interpreter of Paul has to grope his way backward from the finished sentence to *the writing of* it.

30.1. Setting sail in the good ship, Justified Therefore We Have Greenpeace, Paul was blown out of the water by Gallican Judaisers and spent 'a night and a day ... adrift at sea' (2 Cor. 11:25). The name of the vessel was later to become the nucleus of the letter to the Romans.

30.11. It was the letter to the Romans (O'Neill, 1975).

30.2. Paul treats non-Pauline views with contempt. His opponents, in Page's *obiter dictum*, were unable to distinguish the ability to speak from the inability to stop talking. Even if we do not know from Paul what they said, we do know from Paul that they should not have said it.

30.21. But Paul is also confronted by personifying abstractions: 'let not sin therefore reign in your mortal bodies' (Rom.6:12).

30.22. 'Personification requires metaphor ... 'With skeletal hands the trees wrote tales of terror on the sky'' (Ross, 1981, p.151).

30.23. 'Sin' is abstracted from what? From 'gossip', for example (Rom. 1:29 *psithuristēs*, the word is onomatopoeic). But 'gossip' too is abstracted from what was actually whispered in Phoebe's *atrium*, hallway, or court. Paul does not tell us the kind of thing he means, nor give us an instance of the kind of thing he means. What susurrations were there in the pews of Corinth? We hear no more of these than Horace heard of the exchanges of lovers: '... *lenesque sub noctem susurri'* (*Odes* I, IX, 19), their 'gentle whispers in the dark'.

30.24. Paul is confronted not only by persons and personifying abstractions, but by imaginary persons: 'Satan', for example (2 Thess.2:9).

30.25. Now 'Satan' is no more, if no less than a reasonable induction from one half of the 'dialogue of the soul with itself' that a man has between midnight and before the morning watch; or even from the kind of dialogue that one soul has with another soul. Adversarial ideas do not *occur*, it is supposed, to a man, they are *supplied* by an adversary, the calumnies spawned by a calumniator. If 'the mystery of lawlessness is already at work' (2 Thess.2:7), if the political situation is deplorable (what adjective is here strong enough?), if deplorable politicians are already at work, we can be confident that worse will follow.

30.26. The referent of 'Satan' is not to historical agents like Caligula or Agrippa, nor to non-historical agents such as, if different from, God or Jesus, but to a family of phenomena, of which 'the frown of the great' and 'the tyrant's stroke' (Shakespeare: 'Fear no more the heat o' the sun ...') are two; to a family of phenomena which has not been exhaustively explained until all actual and possible negative features of the world have been named. But there is more, for after what is known has been named there remains a sense that no names have been assigned to what remains unknown. There is a *mystery* of iniquity that demands such some notion as *'Unverfügbarkeit'*, 'unmanageability', the sense of a place where 'no service of the feet can serve' (Sophocles, *Oedipus Tyrannus*, 879).

30.3. Those who write about interpretation do not interpret the New Testament and those who interpret the New Testament have no theory. It would be invidious to name the exceptions (e.g. Theissen) that prove the rule. For '(m)ethodolical reflection without exegesis would be empty, exegesis without methodological reflection blind' (Theissen, 1983b, p.40).

30.31. Which is, being interpreted, that they do not interpret. To use a distinction of Gilson (1964, p.11: 'la sagesse différera profondément de l'érudition'), they are erudite, but not philosophical. They do *Historie*, 'history as past, as source', but not *Geschichte*, 'history as significant for the present' (Bultmann, *passim*) and so preclude the posssibility of 'eschatology', a theology that is, that is open to the God 'who is always the coming God' (Bultmann, 1960, p.23 <I thank Mr. P.Balla for locating this reference>).

30.32. The judgement is perfervid, but let it stand; 'leave the *bloody* thing *alone*' (Wittgenstein, cit. Malcolm, 1962, p.85).

30.33. The name, Bultmann, is an exception; though in his great *Theology* he seems curiously reluctant to carry out his own programme: he neither 'demythologises' very much nor existentially interprets very much.

30.34. Does he?

30.35. From the side of the philosophy of interpretation, Ramsey is an exception. But his chapter on biblical language in his *Programmschrift*, 'programmatic essay' (1967, pp.90 ff), is curiously unsatisfactory, though it is difficult to lay one's finger on where the shoe pinches.

30.36. To the task of interpreting the New Testament, ancillary only as that task is (for the main task is to interpret God, and not what other people have said about him; 'oblique orations' are all very well, but can they be a substitute for 'direct speech' <17.2.>?.These lines are a modest contribution, if *apospasmata*, 'fragments', of one kind or another, can be said to deserve the name.

30.37. A.E.Housman (1961, pp.131 ff) has an essay on 'The Application of Thought to Textual Criticism'. This little book is an attempt to apply some fond imagining to the interpretation of Paul of *Tersous*, Tarsus' modern name.

30.4. '... thanks be to God, who in Christ always leads us in triumph' (2 Cor.2:14): When Paul travelled in God's victory parade as a batman-slave in God's chariot he used to (did he?) whisper in God's ear: 'Remember that you are immortal'.

30.41. But perhaps Paul was not *in* the chariot, but running alongside with an amphora full of water to stop the chariot-wheels catching fire, a possibility of which 'Lubrication in Antiquity' reminds us, if we did not know of it before (Harris, 1974). For who can travel safely in a chariot of fire?

30.5. Luke, if we are to trust him, or Acts, if we are to trust them, declares that Paul was a tentmaker (Ac.18:3). A latin recension of a Syriac work, *De sancta cruce* (28,90), if we are to trust it, declares that Paul was a 'scene-painter' ('*exercebat artem scaenografiam*', Nestle, 1892, p.205, cit. Hock, 1980, p.72, fn.8). 'A new occupation for St. Paul', remarks Nestle.

30.51. We recall, if it has happened to us to go to Corinth, for the journey, Horace tells us (*Epistles*, I, XVII, 36), is not for everyman, that the theatre in Corinth could hold 14.000 spectators (Murphy-O'Connor, 1983, p.76; Wiseman, 1979, p.487); and we can imagine, if we want, with what large strokes Paul must have painted with his own hand there, if he did.

30.52. But we must quench the imaginative spirit, for the word translated 'scene-painting' does not prove more than that the Latin editor, Nestle tells us (*op. cit.*), did not know Syriac.

30.53. And yet, just as it was the purpose of the authors of the four Gospels 'to give the truth where possible at once spiritually and corporeally (or outwardly), but where this was not possible, to prefer the spiritual to the corporeal, the true spiritual meaning being often preserved in what at the corporeal level might be called a falsehood' (Origen, *Commentary on St. John's Gospel*, x. 4., cit. Nineham, 1958, p.248), so here, but against the conscious purpose of the editor, the mistranslation may serve to remind us of the large letters with which the theologian *must* and Paul *did* 'word-paint'. Paul's writing is essentially iconic.

30.54. And not Paul's only. 'So we can speak of the Biblical picture as a painting in terms of faith and religious experience and revelation, but a hermeneutical study of the scriptures calls for a literary critical stance and the tools and assumptions of literary criticism to be applied in biblical scholarship' (Dowse, 1986, p.120).

30.6. While it is true that *mutatis mutandis* 'we need to be able to rewrite Amos in order to hear him' (McCaughey, 1986, p.167) it has not been the intention in what is being written here to 'flee awa' ower the buik' (*cit.* Moir I.A., unpublished lecture), in writing *about* Paul to go *beyond* Paul, even if that is where the interpreter of God is bound to go.

30.61. But there is one place where the interpreter of Paul can go beyond him: the interpreter (*quantum mutatus ab illo!*), unlike the apostle in this, can be *both* 'perplexed' *and* 'in despair' (*contra* 2 Cor.4:8). Paul was enabled to manage only one of these — no mean achievement for a man of 'no mean city' (Ac.21:39).

30.7. To be writing something is sometimes to be writing nothing. The view taken here, in Edinburgh, is that Paul, if himself 'nothing' (2 Cor.12:11), was writing something.

30.71. But: ''Write out of me, not out of what you read'' (Dunn, 1985, p.26).

30.72. If we are to follow Paul's example, we should not follow him.

30.73. Just as *Paul* could not 'write out of' the New Testament, twenty-six out of twenty-seven documents of which remained unwritten when he was writing 1 Thessalonians, we should not.

30.74. Reliable writing is done some other way and this is true not only of writing like Paul, but of writing about him, if writing about is different from 'doing', like a recalcitrant schoolboy, Pauline 'lines', sc. making an identical copy of what Paul has already written.

30.75. Writing about is re-writing — just as reading re-writing is re-reading it.

30.8. All men by nature desire.

30.81. All men and women by nature desire one another in one way or another.

30.82. All men and women by nature desire God.

30.9. 'Intellectuals and bureaucrats dilute thought into speech, like a drop of blood into a gallon of water' (Ross, 1981, p.174). Is it true, I ask, that the 'exsanguinated sentence' (Ross, *ibid.*) is *never* true of theologians?

30.91. *Aut tace aut loquere meliora silentio*, 'either be silent or speak things that are better than silence' (legend on Salvator Rosa, Self-portrait <National Gallery, London>, Carroll, *obiter scriptum*).

BIBLIOGRAPHY

Allen W.,
1976,   Without Feathers, London

Angus S.,
1934   Truth and Tradition, Sydney

Auld A.G.,
1983,   'Prophets Through the Looking Glass' and 'Prophets Through the Looking Glass: A Response', JSOT 27.

Barr J.,
1961,   The Semantics of Biblical Language, London

Barrett C.K.,
1964-5,   'Things Sacrified to Idols', NTS 11

1971,   The First Epistle to the Corinthians, London

Barth K.,
1957,   Church Dogmatics, Vol.II, pt.2, Edinburgh

Bentley R.,
1836-8,   Works, ed. Dyce A., London

Betz H.D.,
1979,   Galatians, Philadelphia

Bevan E.,
1962,   Symbolism and Belief, London

Black M(atthew),
1973,   Romans, London

Black M(ax),
1962,   Models and Metaphors, Cornell

1979,   'More about Metaphor', in Ortony A. ed., Metaphor and Thought, Cambridge

Bonhoeffer D.,
1959,   Letters and Papers from Prison, London

1983,   Ethics, 4th imp., re-arranged, London

Boot W.C.,
1979,   'Metaphor as Rhetoric', in Sacks S. ed., On Metaphor, Chicago

Braun H.,
1962,   'Die Indifferenz gegenüber der Welt bei Paulus und bei Epiktet', 'Vom Verstehen des Neuen Testaments' in 'Gesammelte Studien zum Neuen Testament und seiner Umwelt', Tübingen

Briggs C.A.,
1900,   'The use of רוח in the Old Testament', JBL XIX, pt.II

Broneer O.,
1962,   'The Apostle Paul and the Isthmian Games', BA XXV

Browne S.,
1946,   Back from the Front, Edinburgh and London

Buber M.,
1937,   I and Thou, Edinburgh

Bultmann R.,
1910,   Der Stil der paulinischen Predigt und die kynisch-stoische Diatribe, Göttingen

1952,   Theology of the New Testament, Vol. I, London

1953,   'New Testament and Mythology', in: Bartsch H.W. ed., Kerygma and Myth, London

1955,   Theology of the New Testament, Vol. 2, London

1960,   Jesus Christ and Mythology, London

1967,   'Zur Geschichte der Lichtsymbolik im Altertum', in: Exegetica, Tübingen

1976,   Der zweite Brief an die Korinther, Göttingen

Burton E de W.,
1921,   Galatians, Edinburgh

Campbell J.M.,
1959,   The nature of the Atonement, 4th edn., London

Carroll R.,
1983,   'Poets Not Prophets', JSOT 27

Chardin,   cf. Teilhard de Chardin P.

Collingwood R.G.,
1924,   Speculum mentis, Oxford

1933,   An Essay on Philosophical Method, Oxford

1937,   The Principles of Art, Oxford

1939,   An Autobiography, Oxford

1940,   An Essay on Metaphysics, Oxford

1942,   The New Leviathan, Oxford

1944,   An Autobiography, Oxford

Davidson D.,
1979,   'What Metaphors Mean', in Sacks S. ed., On Metaphor, Chicago

Davidson G.R.,
1952,   Corinth: Results of excavations conducted by the American School of Classical Studies at Athens, Vol. XII: The Minor Objects, Princeton.

Davies W.D..
1948,   Paul and Rabbinic Judaism, London

Deas H.T.,
1931,   'The Scholia Vetera to Pindar', Harvard Studies in Classical Philology XLII

Deissmann A.,
1892,   Die neutestamentliche Formel 'in Christo Jesu', Marburg

1927,   Light from the Ancient East, London

Dodd C.H.,
1920,   The Meaning of Paul for Today, London

123

1932,   The Epistle to the Romans, London

1963,   Historical Tradition in the Fourth Gospel, Cambridge

Dodds E.R.,
1973,   The Ancient Concept of Progress, Oxford

Douglas M.,
1973,   Natural Symbols, 2nd ed., London

Dover K.J.,
1954,   'Greek Comedy', in Platnauer M. ed., Fifty Years of Classical
           Scholarship, Oxford

Dowse D.D.,
1986,   'Tillich's Analogia Imaginis: Hermeneutic of Picture and Poetry',
           Encounter, Vol.47, N° 2

Dunn D.,
1985,   Elegies, London

Ebeling G.,
1966,   Wort Gottes und Tradition, 2nd ed., Göttingen

Ebreo L.,
1937,   The Philosophy of Love, trans. Friedeberg-Seeley F. and Barnes
           J.H., London

Edwards G. and Thomson M.,
1970,   'A Hoard of Gold Coins of Philip and Alexander from Corinth', The
           American Journal of Archaeology

Ehrhardt A.,
1964,   The Framework of the New Testament Stories, Manchester

Evans D.D.,
1963,   The Logic of Self-Involvement, London

Farnell L.R.,
1921,   Greek Hero Cults and Ideas of Immortality, Oxford

Farrer A.,
1964,   The Revelation of St. John the Divine, Oxford

Ficino M.,
1944,   Marsilio Ficino's Commentary on Plato's Symposium, ed. Jayne
           S.R., Columbia

Fitzmyer J.A.,
1981,   'Glory Reflected on the Face of Christ (2 Cor.3:7 - 4:6) and a Pales-
           tinian Jewish Motif', TS 42

Foucault M.,
1980,   Power/Knowledge, Brighton

Gadamer H.G.,
1975,   Truth and Method, London

Gale H.M.,
1964,   The Use of Analogy in the Letters of Paul, Philadelphia

Gardner H.,
1965,   The Elegies and the Songs and Sonnets of John Donne, Oxford.

1982,   In Defence of the Imagination, Oxford

Geertz C.,
1968,   'Religion as a Cultural System', in Banton M. ed., Anthropological Approaches to the Study of Religion, London

Gibson J.C.L.,
1979,   'The Last Enemy', SJT, Vol.32, N°2

Gilson E.,
1964,   'Introduction' in Descartes R., Discours de la Méthode, Paris

Gordis R.,
1978,   The Book of Job, New York

Gordon C.,
1980,   in Foucault M., Power/Knowledge, Brighton

Gosse E.,
1916,   Father and Son, London

Grelot P.,
1972,   'Deux expressions difficiles de Philippiens 2,6-7', Biblica 53

Griffith G.T.,
1979,   in Hammond N.G.L. and Griffith G.T., A History of Macedonia, Vol.II, Oxford

Harris H.A.,
1964,   Greek Athletes and Athletics, London

1974,   'Lubrication in Antiquity', Greece and Rome, XXI

Hart R.L.,
1968,   Unfinished Man and the Imagination, New York

Hébert M.,
1899,   Plato and Darwin, London

Heinrici C.F.G.,
1900,   Das zweite Sendschreiben des Apostels Paulus an die Korinthier, 3th ed., Berlin

Henderson I.,
1952,   Myth in the New Testament, London

1967,   Power without Glory, London

Hermann I.,
1961,   Kyrios und Pneuma, München

Hock R.F.,
1980,   The Social Context of Paul's Ministry, Philadelphia

Hooker M.D.,
1980-81, 'Beyond the Things that are Written', NTS 27

Housman A.E.,
1961,   Selected Prose, Cambridge

Janowitz M.,
1963,   'Anthropology and the Social Sciences', Current Anthropology 4:139

Jebb, R.C.,
1892,   The Trachiniae, Cambridge

Jenkins H.,
1982,   Hamlet, London

125

Jeremias J.,
1969,   Jerusalem in the Time of Jesus, London

Jewett R.,
1979,   Dating Paul's Life, London

Jonas H.,
1971,   'Philosophical Meditation on the Seventh Chapter of Paul's Epistle
to the Romans' in Robinson J.M. ed., The Future of Our Religious
Past, London

Jossua J.-P.,
1979,   Un homme cherche Dieu, Paris

Jones R.V.,
1979,   Most Secret War, London

Jowett B.,
1855,   The Epistles of St. Paul to the Thessalonians, Galatians, Romans,
London

Jüngel E.,
1974,   'Metaphorische Wahrheit', Sonderheft zu 'Evangelische Theologie'

Kamlah E.,
1963,   'Wie beurteilt Paulus sein Leiden?', ZNW 54

Käsemann E.,
1969,   New Testament Questions for Today, London

1980,   Commentary on Romans, London

Keck L.E.,
1972,   A Future for the Historical Jesus, London

Kitto H.D.F.,
1951,   The Greeks, London

Knox W.L.,
1932,   St. Paul, London

1939,   St. Paul and the Church of the Gentiles, Cambridge

Körner J.,
1957,   Eschatologie und Geschichte, Hamburg

Lakoff G. and Johnson M.,
1980,   Metaphors We Live By, Chicago

Lambrecht J.,
1983,   'Structure and Line of Thought in 2 Cor.2,14-4,6', Biblica 64

Loisy A.F.,
1903,   Autour d'un petit livre, 2nd ed., Paris

1931,   Mémoires, Vol. 2, Paris

1933,   La Naissance du Christianisme, Paris

1935,   Remarques sur la littérature épistolaire du Nouveau Testament,
Paris

1948,   The Birth of the Christian Religion, London

Lonergan B.J.F.,
1972,   Method in Theology, London

Lucas J.,
1970,   The Freedom of the Will, Oxford

1976,   Freedom and Grace, London

Lynch W.F.,
1970,   Christ and Prometheus, Notre Dame

McCaughey J.D.,
1986,   'Imagination in the Understanding of the Prophets', in Mackey J.P. ed., Religious Imagination, Edinburgh

McDonald A.H.,
1954,   'The Roman Historians', in Platnauer M. ed., Fifty Years of Classical Scholarship, Oxford

Mackinnon D.M.,
1963,   'Moral Objections', in Objections to Christian Belief, London

1974,   The Problem of Metaphysics, Cambridge

Maier G.,
1977,   The End of the Historical Critical Method, St. Louis

Malcolm N. and Wright G.H.v.,
1962,   Ludwig Wittgenstein – A Memoir, Oxford

Manson T.W.,
1949,   The Sayings of Jesus, London

Marett R.R.,
1932,   Faith, Hope and Charity in Primitive Religion, Oxford

1933,   Sacraments of Simple Folk, Oxford

Martin A.,
1984,   Kintyre, Edinburgh

Martin G.D.,
1975,   Language, Truth and Poetry, Edinburgh

Matheson P.C.,
1979,   'Yesterday's Reformation Today', Theology 82

Maxwell R.,
1943,   Still Point, London

Morgan R.,
1973,   The Nature of New Testament Theology, London

Moule C.F.D.,
1963,   An Idiom-Book of New Testament Greek, 2nd ed., Cambridge

1972,   '2 Cor 3:18b, καθάπερ ἀπὸ κυρίου πνεύματος', in Baltensweiler H. and Reicke B. eds., Neues Testament und Geschichte, Zürich-Tübingen

Murphy-O'Connor J.,
1976,   'Christological Anthropology in Phil. II,6-11', RB 83

1983,   St. Paul's Corinth, Wilmington

Neil W.,
1967,   The Letter of Paul to the Galatians, Cambridge

Nestle E.,
1892,   'St. Paul's Handicraft: Acts XVIII. 3', JBL, Vol.XI, Part II

Nineham D.E.,
1958,   'Eyewitness Testimony and the Gospel Tradition, II', JTS, N.S.9

1963,   The Church's Use of the Bible, London

Nock A.D.,
    1964,   Early Gentile Christianity and its Hellenistic Background, New York

    1972,   Essays on Religion and the Ancient World, Vols. I and II, Oxford

Nowottny W.,
    1965,   The Language Poets Use, London

Ogden S.M.,
    1962,   Christ without Myth, London

    1982,   The Point of Christology, London

Oman J.,
    1917,   Grace and Personality, Cambridge

O'Neill J.C.,
    1975,   Paul's ostcrad to the Romans, London

Paton H.J.,
    1955,   The Modern Predicament, London

Patte D.,
    1983,   Paul's Faith and the Power of the Gospel, Philadelphia

Proudfoot G.R. ed.,
    1970,   The Two Noble Kinsmen, London

Rad G. von,
    1958,   Gesammelte Studien zum Alten Testament, München

    1975,   Old Testament Theology, London

Ramsey I.T.,
    1964,   Models and Mystery, London

    1965,   'Contemporary Philosophy and the Christian Faith', RS 1, N° 1

    1966,   'Talking about God', in Dillistone F.W. ed., Myth and Symbol, London

    1967,   Religious Language, London

    1969   Freedom and Immortality, London

    1973 a,   'The Crisis of Faith', Theoria to Theory, 7

    1973 b,   Models for Divine Activity, London

    1974,   Christian Empiricism, Gill J.H. ed., London

Renan E.,
    1869,   Histoire des Origines du Christianisme, Vol.3: Saint Paul, Paris

Ricoeur P.,
    1969,   The Symbolism of Evil, New York

    1978,   The Rule of Metaphor, London

    1981,   Essays on Biblical Interpretation, London

Rohde E.,
    1925,   Psyche, 8th edn., trans. Hillis W.B., London

Ross J.F.,
    1969,   Introduction to the Philosophy of Religion, London

    1981,   Portraying Analogy, Cambridge

Sanday W. and Headlam A.C.,
    1902.   The Epistle to the Romans, 5th edn., Edinburgh

Sanders E.P.,
1977,   Paul and Palestinian Judaism, London

Schlier H.,
1971,   Der Brief an die Galater, 5th edn., Göttingen

Schon D.A.,
1963,   The Displacement of Concepts, London

Schütz J.H.,
1975,   Paul and the Anatomy of Apostolic Authority, Cambridge

Schweitzer A.,
1911,   The Quest of the Historical Jesus, London

Scranton R.L.,
1951,   Corinth: Results of Excavations conducted by the American School
          of Classical Studies at Athens, Vol.I, Part III, Princeton

Smith G.A.,
1894,   The Historical Geography of the Holy Land, London

Smith R. Gregor,
1956,   The New Man, London

1960,   J.G.Hamann, London

1966,   Secular Christianity, London

1969,   The Free Man, London

1970,   The Doctrine of God, London

Stanford W.B.,
1936,   Greek Metaphor, Oxford

Steinberg L.,
1953,   'The eye is Part of the Mind', Partisan Review 70

1984,   The Sexuality of Christ in Renaissance Art and in Modern Oblivion,
          London

Stewart J.S.,
1935,   A Man in Christ, London

Straub W.,
1937,   Die Bildersprache des Apostels Paulus, Tübingen

Tennant F.R.,
1928-30, Philosophical Theology, Vols. I and II, Cambridge

Teilhard de Chardin P.,
1959,   The Phenomenon of Man, London

1960,   Le Milieu Divin, London

Templeton E.A.,
1978,   'On Undoing the Past', (unpublished) Paper to the Society for the
          Study of Theology

Theissen G.,
1974,   'Soteriologische Symbolik in den paulinischen Schriften', KuD 20

1983a,   Psychologische Aspekte paulinischer Theologie, Göttingen

1983b,   Miracle Stories of the Early Christian Tradition, Edinburgh

Tillich P.,
1961a,   'The Religious Symbol', in Hook S. ed., Experience and Truth, New
          York

1961b, 'The Meaning and Justification of Religious Symbols', in Hook S. ed., Experience and Truth, New York

Tracy D.,
1979, 'Metaphor and Religion', in Sacks S. ed., On Metaphor, Chicago and London

Turner V.,
1970, The Forest of Symbols, London

1974, Dramas, Fields and Metaphors, New York

Turner V. and Turner E.,
1978, Image and Pilgrimage in Christian Culture, Oxford

van Buren P.M.,
1963, The Secular Meaning of the Gospel, London

Vaux R.de,
1961, Ancient Israel, London

Vermes G.,
1973, Jesus the Jew, London

1981, The Gospel of Jesus the Jew, Newcastle upon Tyne

Vidler A.R.,
1970, A Variety of Catholic Modernists, Cambridge

Weitz M.,
1965, Hamlet and the Philosophy of Literary Criticism, London

Wheelwright P.,
1968, The Burning Fountain, rev. edn., Indiana

Whitehead A.N.,
1926, Religion in the Making, Cambridge

1979, Process and Reality, corrected edn., New York

Wilamowitz-Möllendorf U. von,
1905, Die griechische und lateinische Literatur und Sprache, Berlin

Wilder A.N.,
1976, Theopoetic, Philadelphia

1982, Jesus' Parables and the War of Myths, London

Wisdom J.,
1953, Philosophy and Psycho-analysis, Oxford

Wiseman J.,
1979, 'Corinth and Rome, I: 228 B.C. - A.D. 267', in Temporini H. ed., Aufstieg und Niedergang der römischen Welt, Berlin

Wittgenstein L.,
1958, Philosophical Investigations, 2nd edn., Oxford

1978, Lectures and Conversations on Aesthetics, Psychology and Religious Belief, Oxford

Woods G.F.,
1958, Theological Explanation, Welwyn

Zuurdeeg W.F.,
1959, An Analytical Philosophy of Religion, London

τί δῆθ' ὁ πρωκτὸς ἐς τὸν οὐρανὸν βλέπει;

(Aristophanes, *The Clouds*, 193)

'Then why's their rump turned up towards the sky?'
or
'Is the best theological method a Posterior Analytic?'

'There is very little mother-wit in the world,
but a great deal of clergy.'

(Sydney Smith to Lord Holland, 1815)